T0316598

# Cambridge Elements ≡

**Elements in American Politics**
edited by
Frances E. Lee
*Princeton University*

# THE FULL ARMOR OF GOD

## *The Mobilization of Christian Nationalism in American Politics*

Paul A. Djupe
*Denison University*

Andrew R. Lewis
*University of Cincinnati*

Anand E. Sokhey
*University of Colorado, Boulder*

Shaftesbury Road, Cambridge CB2 8EA, United Kingdom

One Liberty Plaza, 20th Floor, New York, NY 10006, USA

477 Williamstown Road, Port Melbourne, VIC 3207, Australia

314–321, 3rd Floor, Plot 3, Splendor Forum, Jasola District Centre,
New Delhi – 110025, India

103 Penang Road, #05–06/07, Visioncrest Commercial, Singapore 238467

Cambridge University Press is part of Cambridge University Press & Assessment,
a department of the University of Cambridge.

We share the University's mission to contribute to society through the pursuit of
education, learning and research at the highest international levels of excellence.

www.cambridge.org
Information on this title: www.cambridge.org/9781009423922

DOI: 10.1017/9781009234078

First published 2023

A catalogue record for this publication is available from the British Library.

ISBN 978-1-009-42392-2 Hardback
ISBN 978-1-009-23406-1 Paperback
ISSN 2515-1606 (online)
ISSN 2515-1592 (print)

# The Full Armor of God

## The Mobilization of Christian Nationalism in American Politics

Elements in American Politics

DOI: 10.1017/9781009234078
First published online: June 2023

Paul A. Djupe
*Denison University*

Andrew R. Lewis
*University of Cincinnati*

Anand E. Sokhey
*University of Colorado, Boulder*

**Author for correspondence:** Paul A. Djupe, djupe@denison.edu

**Abstract:** Academic research on Christian nationalism (CN) has revealed a considerable amount about the scope of its relationships to public policy views in the United States. However, work thus far has not addressed an essential question: Why now? Research by the authors of this Element advances answers, showcasing how deeper engagement with "the 3 Ms" – measurement, mechanisms, and mobilization – can help unpack how and why CN has entered our politics as a partisan project. Indeed, it is difficult to understand the dynamics of CN without reference to the parties, as it has been a worldview used to mobilize Republicans while simultaneously recruiting and demobilizing Democrats. The mechanisms of these efforts hinge on a deep desire for social dominance that is ordained by God – an order elites suggest is threatened by Democrats and "the left." These elite appeals can have sweeping consequences for opinion and action, including the public's support for democratic processes.

**Keywords:** Christian nationalism, partisanship, polarization, tolerance, persecution beliefs

ISBNs: 9781009423922 (HB), 9781009234061 (PB), 9781009234078 (OC)
ISSNs: 2515-1606 (online), 2515-1592 (print)

# Contents

1  What We Don't Understand about Christian
   Nationalism in the United States and Why
   It Matters                                                    1

2  The Fundamentals: Measurement and the Precursors
   to Mobilization                                               9

3  Christian Nationalism as Partisan Mobilization               17

4  Mobilizing a Threatened Worldview into Politics              30

5  Christian Nationalist Tensions with Democracy                44

6  Conclusion: Putting Christian Nationalism
   in Context                                                    62

   References                                                    69

## 1 What We Don't Understand about Christian Nationalism in the United States and Why It Matters

In the summer of 2022, a select committee in the House of Representatives held hearings on the January 6, 2021, Insurrection at the Capitol. Chairperson Benny Thompson (D-MS) opened proceedings on June 9, 2022, making it clear that the committee found that former President Donald Trump conspired to overturn the results of the 2020 presidential election in an "attempted coup." But President Trump did not act alone. In the middle of the first day of hearings, the committee played a video of the violent insurrection, overlaid with President Trump imploring Vice President Mike Pence "to do the right thing." Among the insurrectionists were Proud Boys and QAnon Shamans, white nationalists, and Trump loyalists. As they breached security and invaded the Capitol rotunda shouting "Whose House? Our House!", the iconography was potent. People were clad with Make America Great Again (MAGA) paraphernalia, Confederate flags, and a host of white nationalist symbols. Many infused Christianity into their efforts to overturn the democratic process.

As journalist Emma Green described it, "The name of God was everywhere during Wednesday's insurrection against the American government" (Green 2021). Crosses were scattered throughout the mob scene. One woman declared, "Here we are in the name of Jesus," as she broke into the Capitol building (Boorstein 2021). "We were founded as a Christian country. And we see how far we have come from that," one rioter exclaimed on her Facebook Live feed (Jenkins 2022). A Christian flag, with its white background and blue upper left canton layered with a simple red Latin cross, was paraded around the House of Representatives (Winston 2021).

Christianity was being used to solemnize the insurrection, and this had become a common theme among Trump's most vocal supporters. Just hours earlier, Paula White, Trump's spiritual advisor, prayed at the Save America rally where Trump would soon rile up supporters by threatening Pence. White repeated "Today, let justice be done" three times in the middle of her five minute prayer, adding, "Let we the people have the assurance of a fair and just election" (C-SPAN 2022).

Weeks prior, Trump's leading religious supporters organized a series of Jericho Marches, based on the Old Testament story of the fall of Jericho in Joshua 6, where the Israelites prayed and marched around the city seven times. On the march, the Israelites blew a horn (the shofar), and the walls of Jericho fell. Trump supporters were hoping for the collapse of the 2020 election results. In an official statement, the Jericho March organizers declared: "Vice President Pence has the ability to elect the President himself and Jericho March calls on him to exercise his rightful power in the face of the blatant fraud and corruption." On January 5 and 6, the Jericho March again descended on Washington, DC, with a plan to march around the Supreme Court on January 5 and the US Capitol on January 6 (Smietana 2021). The marchers were a key cog in the January 6 movement to overturn the election. As Thomas Lecaque wrote at The Bulwark, "And after re-enacting the Book of Joshua, when the walls of the Capitol didn't come down, Trump's supporters decided to go over them instead" (Lecaque 2022).

Some headlines were quick to label January 6, 2021, events at the US Capitol a "Christian Insurrection" (Green 2021) and "Christian nationalism" (CN) (Edsall 2021), building on academic scholarship that has pinpointed CN as a leading explanation for the rise of Trump and a host of culture war issues (Gorski and Perry 2022; Stewart 2020; Whitehead and Perry 2020a).

But Christian nationalism did not act alone. The now standard academic story about CN misses critical lessons from political science about mobilization. Much of the scholarship about CN focuses on public opinion and how Christian nationalist views are connected to issue attitudes (see e.g., Whitehead and Perry 2020a), while a separate subset has drawn attention to organizations, philosophies, and elite discourse (see e.g., Stewart 2020; Gorski 2017). However, these streams need to be combined in order to document the processes that link public opinion with political behavior through mobilization. To understand the influence of CN, we will focus on mechanisms that activate this worldview, which is and has been quite prevalent within the general public. Along the way we will also scrutinize the measurement of the concept itself. Focusing on just one of these elements to the exclusion of others risks missing the big picture: January 6 did not happen simply because of a prevalent worldview – it had to be mobilized by elites and organizations who have laid the groundwork for political action. Christian nationalism is and has been a partisan project.

Trump's engagement with Christian nationalist rhetoric highlights several potential mechanisms to which we will give close attention. As the House Committee held hearings on Trump's role in the insurrection in 2022, he continued to court conservative Christians. A day after the Committee heard testimony that Trump's lawyer John Eastman had sought a pardon for advocating Vice President Pence overturn the 2020 election, Trump gave an address at the Faith and Freedom Coalition – an annual meeting of Christian Right activists. "Remember, in the end, they are not after me. They are after you. That's true. They're after you. They're after everything we stand for," Trump declared (S. Davis 2022). Most in the crowd surely subscribed to the core tenets of CN – they were at a conference called Faith and Freedom, afterall. But *threat* was what Trump used to activate them. Democrats were threatening the country and Christianity then; they did it again with the FBI's raid on Mar-a-Lago. This emphasis on threat is one of the key ways in which Christian nationalism is mobilized to endanger democracy.

By emphasizing threats, conservative elites mobilize CN into politics. Threat is one of the most powerful motivational forces, but it is a dangerous one because it often suggests that opponents are straying outside the bounds of democratic politics. As we will show in this Element, the CN we should be concerned with has largely been mobilized with the threat of Christian persecution (CP), which justifies all manner of prejudicial policies and antidemocratic actions, including the January 6 Insurrection.

Before we dive into the components of our broader argument about the mobilization of CN, we first take a few pages to set the stage. In the remainder of this introduction we begin by defining CN before discussing in more detail why a new, more comprehensive approach is needed to better understand its effects. Finally, we provide the plan for the Element.

## 1.1 What Is Christian Nationalism?

Christian nationalism refers to a set of beliefs that the nation is of, by, and for Christians. Gorski describes it as a "sort of apocalyptic and nativistic hyperpatriotism" (2017, p. viii), and Whitehead and Perry describe it as an "ideology that idealizes and advocates a fusion of American civic life with a particular type of Christian identity and culture" (2020a, p. x).

When we discuss CN we prefer the term "worldview" because it more appropriately captures the set of beliefs as well as values that drive opinions and actions on behalf of Christians. It is an exclusivist orientation – a societal boundary – separating groups who do not belong and uniting those that do (see also Edgell et al. 2006; Taylor 2002). Christian nationalism extends from a past imbued with rightful social relations dominated by a Christian majority into an uncertain future where a Christian minority is threatened by non- and anti-Christian foes. As Lewis describes, "Christian nationalism demarcates who we were and who we should be. It is retrospective to an idealized American religious founding and prospective toward recovering 'one nation under God'" (Lewis 2021: 111–112).

Christian nationalism, therefore, defines citizenship narrowly on a group-basis; it articulates the right aims for public policy, which are to work overtly to benefit Christian groups and individuals. The right groups – Christians – are elevated, while outsiders are marginalized. This can manifest through negative feelings toward out-groups, perceptions of threat, and discriminatory policy.

Christian nationalism is different from patriotism and civil religion. First, patriotism differs from nationalism, because while it inspires bonds, loyalty, and love of country, it is not marked by exclusivity and boundary marking (Smith 2021). Although there is overlap, nationalism is typically focused on ethnic ties; patriotism is focused on the broader and more inclusive political community (Primoratz 2020). Civil religion, meanwhile, emphasizes transcendent values of the political community, giving political symbols, events, and narratives the features of religion – the goal is bringing together a diverse people around common commitments and symbols (Bellah 1967; Gorski 2017). Thus, while civil religion and patriotism seek unity, CN emphasizes internal boundaries and divides a nation along religious lines. McDaniel, Nooruddin, and Shortle (2022) provide a helpful discussion of these distinctions as they investigate the origins and consequences of a related concept, American religious exceptionalism (ARE).

## 1.2 When? Which? Who? The Need for Mechanisms

Research investigating the relationship between CN and political behavior has exploded over the past decade, looking at its correlates with varied outcomes. Christian nationalism has been linked to – among other things – opinions regarding police mistreatment of African Americans (Perry et al. 2019), opposition to gun control (Whitehead et al. 2018), opposition to immigration (McDaniel et al., 2011; Sherkat and Lehman 2018; Shortle and Gaddie 2015), opposition to same-sex marriage (Whitehead and Perry 2015), opposition to COVID-19 vaccinations (Whitehead and Perry 2020b), votes for Donald Trump (Baker et al. 2020a), and support for the January 6 Insurrection (Armaly et al. 2022a; Gorski and Perry 2022). Most of the work has emphasized CN's religious and political boundary marking (see Whitehead and Perry 2020a), though some efforts have emphasized racial dimensions (Baker et al. 2020b; Jones 2021; Gorski and Perry 2022; McDaniel et al. 2022). Gorski and Perry (2022, 17) write that "the deep story and political vision of Christian nationalism is whiteness."

Clearly, existing work documents an enormous array of linkages to public policy and intergroups relations, but there are steps yet untaken regarding why those relationships hold now and how they matter for political action. In prior scholarship, CN is typically interpreted as being the most important driver of individual-level effects. For example, Whitehead and Perry write, "Simply put, knowing if you are an Ambassador or Rejector of Christian nationalism can now tell us far more about your social and political views than knowing what denomination you affiliate with, how often you attend church, and even whether you identify as Democrat or Republican" (2020a, 44). It is quite plausible, however, that CN is a proxy for other items that are correlated with the index – and/or that loading statistical models with several related items is obscuring forces at play.

This points to a problem with most existing work on CN: there is a paucity of evidence of the mechanisms driving CN effects, which limits the ability to establish the influence of CN relative to other factors. One study does this quite well, arguing that "Christian nationalism is likely to be conditioned by other individual characteristics that scholars have identified as particularly susceptible to elite cues," including threat perception and perceived victimhood (Armaly et al. 2022a). Yet, it does so with a single dataset, analyzing a few, but, important mechanisms. This is simply to say that there is more work to be done in this regard.

Relatedly, many studies pay lip service to partisanship, while downplaying its role to activate and structure CN beliefs. Typically, CN beliefs are added to a model with partisanship, ideology, and a host of demographic factors. When CN has a large effect, it is interpreted that it is more important than partisanship (e.g., Whitehead and Perry 2020a, 12). In other places, authors argue that CN is "one of the main drivers of political polarization" (Gorski and Perry 2022, 28). Yet, the partisan connections to CN (and polarization) are not directly tested. Christian nationalism scholarship also, appropriately, makes claims about elite opinion leadership and influence without measuring elite connections to mass political behavior. For example, Gorski and Perry claim that white CN is a "dog whistle" that CN elites used to prime mass response (Gorski and Perry 2022, 41), a position we take as well, but those mechanisms are not tested directly by their data.

What is needed are direct tests of the potential mechanisms that activate the influence of CN, a direction consistent with the religious communication approach, in which measures of exposure to information and its adoption are necessary in order to understand the causal role of religion (see e.g., Djupe and Neiheisel 2022a). This will help build confidence in relationships as well as refine understandings of the effects of holding the CN worldview. Importantly, there is no explicit inclusion of mobilization in most scholarship that links CN with political behavior. If we know that CN is a widely held disposition that has been present for some time in American politics (Whitehead and Perry 2020a), then our theory and research should be able to answer a critical question – Why now?

## 1.3 Our Approach: The 3 Ms

To analyze the influence of CN in American politics, we look at three factors – what we call the 3 Ms: (1) the measurement of the worldview and how choices in measurement and statistical modeling affect interpretations (see e.g., Achen

2002; N. Davis 2022); (2) the mobilization from elite actors and organizations, following scholarship that investigates public opinion leadership (e.g., Lupia and McCubbins 1998; Zaller 1992); (3) the underlying mechanisms of Christian nationalist opinion formation, seeking to tease out the political psychology that is linked to, and activated by, the worldview (see e.g., Armaly et al. 2022a; Pratto et al. 1994).

By focusing on the 3 Ms (measurement, mobilization to action, and mechanisms of opinion formation), our goal is to bring greater understanding to how CN works in American politics. We investigate assumptions that scholars make about why CN is an important part of our politics, showing what the connections are and how they are (or are not) linked to other forces.

The mobilization of the Christian nationalist worldview to action takes center stage. Not long ago, CN was the simple conflation of majority religion with the state and was largely sidelined in analyses of American politics. In fact, one recent comparative analysis of religious nationalism argued, strikingly, that the institutional structure of the United States prevented CN from taking hold (Soper and Fetzer 2018; cf. McDaniel et al. 2022, ch. 1). In at least the last few decades, however, this worldview has been mobilized and polarized in service of the political success of the Republican Party – a project that has been quite successful. While we are interested in documenting the relationship between CN and public policy and intergroup relations, our primary focus is on the role that political and psychological forces play in mobilizing Christian nationalists. When available, we analyze these connections over time.

A considerable amount of the work of documenting the links of CN to policy attitudes has been done, and the literature continues to expand. However, the existing research is incomplete; often it ignores (or merely assumes) the special roles played by elites, the parties and partisanship, and other political psychological factors, like social dominance orientation (SDO), that lay the groundwork for Christian nationalists to view policies and people in particular ways that align with group threat and interests.

One can easily quibble about the exact list of oversights in the literature, but at base it involves fundamental questions of *when*, *which*, and *who*: When is CN likely to be active in American politics? Which Christian nationalists are likely to take action?[1] And, who are the actors most likely to spark

---

[1] Following others (e.g., Whitehead and Perry 2020b), we mostly measure Christian nationalism via an index of items. This yields a continuous measure of the concept, and individuals present scores across its full range. We mostly avoid using cut points of this index in our analyses, as we want to use as much information as possible and avoid producing insights that are sensitive to such potentially arbitrary choices. This means that there is no specific threshold that delineates a Christian nationalist from others, though we will sometimes mark the most and least ardent supporters by the first and fourth quartiles. Practically speaking, however, when we note

mobilization? That is, CN could return to a de facto dormant state if it were not for credible elites continuing to cue believers with a broad slate of threats. Moreover, given the degree of polarization in American politics, Christian nationalist cue givers are largely sorted by partisanship and have as a central and shared goal funneling more votes toward the Republican Party. Thus, the connections of CN to policy issues should be understood as a partisan project. Before we proceed, however, a quick word about our data sources.

## 1.4 The Data We Use

To test our claims we need data that span time and include items on policy issues, CN, Christian persecution beliefs, partisanship, orientations toward elites, and political participation. These requirements are met by a range of data, including long-running clergy surveys, original surveys conducted by the authors, and existing omnibus surveys, that we use to triangulate our conceptualization of how CN has been mobilized. As data appear, we provide brief overviews and footnotes with more information. We draw on evidence from five source types:

1. A long-running survey of evangelical clergy from the Southern Baptist Convention (SBC), collected every four years from 1988 to 2008 by James Guth to show the early distribution of CN and partisanship among Christian elites.
2. Baylor Religion Surveys (Wave II, Wave V (2007, 2017)) on CN in the mass public over time.
3. Democracy Fund Voter Study Group panel data, showing Christian nationalists moving toward the Republican Party.
4. Seven national sample surveys fielded by the authors between 2018 and 2022 investigating links between CN, threat, and partisanship.
5. Panel data from 2016 (fielded by a subset of the authors), permitting investigations of CN and orientations toward elite messaging.

Unless otherwise noted, the model-based evidence that follows comes from ordinary least squares regressions with controls for race, age, education, gender, partisanship, attendance, and religious tradition. In visualizations, comparisons of any two confidence intervals are equivalent to a 90 percent test at the point of overlap.

---

relationships and discuss "Christian nationalists," we are referring to individuals scoring on the higher end of the scale.

## 1.5 The Plan of the Element

In Section 2 we begin by delving into two of the Ms – measurement and mobilization. We open by examining and experimenting with well-known measures of CN, noting what they seem to capture versus alternatives. We then look at the precursors to mobilization by seeing whether elite support for CN in the United States preceded public movement and documenting the extent to which CN has sorted on partisan lines.

In Section 3 we focus on mobilization into action via the essential and complicated relationship between CN and the parties, particularly the GOP. One of the surprising things we will show is the weakening effect of CN on policy attitudes among Republicans over time, which indicates that the party has been effectively captured by CN – most Republicans now take stands that resemble Christian nationalist positions even when they do not hold strident CN beliefs. At the same time, CN cross-pressures Democrats, bringing them toward Republican positions. Because of this, CN is an effective framework for Republicans and a difficult one for Democrats to counter.

As mechanisms of opinion formation are another important part of our story, we explore these issues in Section 4. Here, we find that not all Christian nationalists have aspirations of taking power and implementing exclusive, pro-Christian policies. Rather, the ones who seem to desire this appear to be distinctive in two respects: they score high on SDO, and they receive cues from right-wing elites at higher rates.

But are Christian nationalists playing for keeps, mobilized by a threat that suggests all is at stake with the other side backed by evil forces? Processes that would allow evil access to power should be opposed to help guarantee the right answer. That is, just as others have documented tensions with science (Perry et al. 2021), in Section 5 we explore Christian nationalists' tensions with democracy. Among other things, we observe that they are more intolerant, are less likely to reject some less-democratic processes and alternatives (see also McDaniel et al. 2022), and express more support for extremist groups – all of these things are motivated by greater perceived threat.

In the conclusion we recap what we've found and speculate on the future of CN. We discuss whether and how religious organizations support its adoption, as well as attempts among some organizations to reject it. While evangelicalism has taken a reputational hit for adopting such a brazen worldview, many non-evangelical conservatives have flocked to the evangelical label as a result (Burge 2021). We suspect that CN will remain a part of American politics well into the future, though there's always the chance that it may become dormant again. Regardless, in its present incarnation there is ample evidence that CN poses a threat to democratic process and practice in the United States.

## 2 The Fundamentals: Measurement and the Precursors to Mobilization

In this section we share our first empirics as we evaluate typical measures of CN against several alternatives. We open with measurement because if we're going to build on others' advances, we need to be confident that previous efforts have been accurately capturing the core concept. We then shift our attention to assessing support for dynamics that should accompany a story of partisan mobilization as it pertains to opinion and action (our focus in Sections 3–6) – that is, we look to see whether we can document early movement by elites and whether there seem to be wells of partisan support for Christian nationalist ideas waiting for activation.

### 2.1 Operationalizing Christian Nationalism

In public opinion research, CN has been measured with a few different strategies. By far, the most prominent approach – and the one we focus on subsequently – is the CN scale employed by Andrew Whitehead and Samuel Perry (see Whitehead and Perry 2020a). The scale is made up of five or six survey questions that originated in the Baylor Religion Survey beginning in Wave II (2007). Each item captures the degree of vestment of Christianity in the nation and the government, though several are vague about who benefits. These items are (with the orientation of the high value in parentheses):

- The federal government should declare the United States a Christian nation (agree)
- The federal government should advocate Christian values (agree)
- The federal government should enforce strict separation of church and state (disagree)
- The federal government should allow the display of religious symbols in public spaces (agree)
- The success of the United States is part of God's plan (agree)
- The federal government should allow prayer in public schools (agree).

It is important to note that others have put forth scales with different emphases. For example, McDaniel, Nooruddin, and Shortle (2022) develop a measure of "American religious exceptionalism" (ARE); they use up to four questions for this, only one of which directly overlaps with the Whitehead and Perry (2020b) approach: "America holds a special place in God's plan," "The success of the

US is not a reflection of divine will," "The US is spiritually predestined to lead the world," and "The vast resources of the US indicate that God has chosen it to lead other nations" (McDaniel et al. 2022: 51). The ARE items focus more on the United States relative to the world, and neither specify how the United States should be constituted nor gauge individuals' support for specific policies on church-state questions. Scores on this ARE scale do appear to be well correlated with the Baylor CN scale ($r = 0.73$ in our September 2021 survey), though we would not consider them to be substitutable. McDaniel et al. (2022) themselves treat the CN items as distinct "attitudes about the religious roots of the nation and religious groups" – they use the ARE battery to predict who the public thinks should be part of the country ("National Content"), as gauged via some of the CN items (2022: 92–93). We encourage future scholarship to more closely examine the similarities and differences in how these two measures structure a range of attitudes and behaviors.

Because Whitehead and Perry's CN scale has gained so much scholarly attention, we included it on a number of our surveys. In the sections that follow we primarily replicate and engage with versions of their scale. That said, we also examine original items we have fielded since 2016. Some of our studies only contained five of the six items previously noted (omitting the public display of religious symbols item), though this has little impact on the scale's distribution or function as we have found.

While the Whitehead and Perry CN scale has become a nearly ubiquitous way to measure the worldview of CN, some scholars have critiqued its validity (e.g., Lewis 2021). Nicholas Davis provides the most thorough examination, concluding that the multi-item scale "jams together" several ideas that are "theoretically and empirically separable" (N. Davis 2022: 25). Instead, Davis suggests that the Christian nation and Christian values items best represent CN and urges scholars to only use those two.

We have heeded this warning and investigated some of the effects of scale construction. The correlations between various configurations of the index are very high: 0.83 between the Christian nation item and the six-item index, 0.89 for the Christian nation and Christian values items and the full index, and 0.96 between the four items minus the school prayer and church and state items and the full index (our September 2021 data). In Figure 1, we compare the effects of variations of the CN scale on multiple dependent variables. While there are minor differences, the effects are quite consistent, with only small variations. In the case of political activity, there is no significant variation across indices. Across all, the one and two item indices have the weakest estimated effects, perhaps because a full point move on the larger scales means movement across multiple variables. Buoyed by this evidence, we use the full (five or six items,

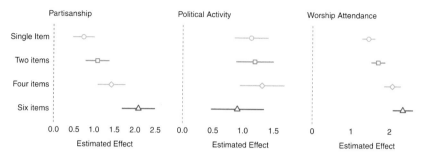

**Figure 1** Does Christian nationalist index construction make a difference? Comparing index composition effects across three dependent variables (September 2021)

depending on the survey) index going forward, mostly for the sake of comparability. In two cases, we use a single "Christian nation" item in the absence of the other questions. But, we encourage scholars to continue to pursue investigations into the validity of the items and the dimensionality of CN.

## 2.2 CN as a Worldview? Evaluating the Stability of Christian Nationalism

Previously we noted that we prefer to think of CN as a "worldview"; this term captures the idea of a set of beliefs and values that drive opinions and actions on behalf of Christians. But if we're going to think of CN in these terms, we need some evidence that CN orientations are stable. Thus, we attempt to assess CN's stability in two ways.

### 2.2.1 Do CN Measures Respond to Trump-Era Rhetoric?

First, we want to see if the aggressive rhetoric of the Trump years spurred people to adopt greater Christian nationalist worldviews. In our July 2021 survey (so, late in the game), we randomly assigned one of three treatments (or a pure control that asked for state residency). Each of these treatments began similarly: "Christian symbols and language were highly visible at the January 6th, 2021 attack on the US Capitol: huge crosses, people blowing ram's horns, and flags." However, the conditions then diverged:

– The first condition drew on Tony Perkins' excuse for his support for Trump after the Stormy Daniels affair was made known (qtd. in McAfee 2018): "One participant justified the attack this way: You know, you only have two cheeks. Look, Christianity is not all about being a welcome mat which people can just stomp their feet on."

– The second was more aggressive, quoting infamous pastor Greg Locke (qtd. in Edsall 2021):

> One participant justified the attack this way: We are one election away from losing everything we hold dear. The battle is against everything evil and wicked in the world. It is a rallying of the troops of God's holy army. This is our day. This is our time. This means something for the Kingdom. As a matter of fact, THIS MEANS WAR (emphasis in the original).

– The third took the opposite tack, quoting a theology professor at Gardner-Webb Divinity School: "Minister friends, we must confront directly the baseless conspiracy theories and allegations that our own church members are embracing and passing along. They are not just wrongheaded ideas; they have disastrous consequences for democracy, and to tie these falsehoods to the salvation of Jesus is nothing less than blasphemy" (qtd. in Wingfield 2021).

Did these primes affect CN scores? Figure 2 presents the CN scale scores for evangelicals and non-evangelical identifiers by partisanship across these conditions. Overall, we find effectively no treatment effects. For instance, among pure independents, the "confront" treatment has a negative effect weakening CN slightly, but the "this means war" treatment effect is also negative (and they should be opposites). In no treatment do evangelicals post different CN scores compared to the control, and only in one case does the non-evangelical group differ from the control (Tony Perkins' rejection of turning the other cheek), where the CN score is significantly lower. From these results, CN looks to be a stable worldview.

### 2.2.2 Are CN Measures Christian Enough?

We try a second tack at stability by addressing a frequent twitter criticism muttered – that the wording of the Baylor CN items is not particularly Christian nationalist. As the critique frequently goes, the federal government's promotion

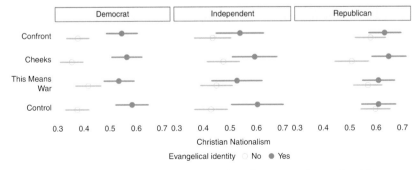

**Figure 2** The stability of Christian nationalism, experimental evidence (July 2021)

of Christian values encompasses loving thy neighbor and is therefore not exclusive to Christians. Accordingly, we randomly assigned two different CN scales, one of which used the original wording, and the other which used more explicitly exclusive language. Specifically, we altered three of the items (the changes are bolded), leaving the other two unchanged:

- The federal government should advocate Christian values **for the benefit of Christians**.
- The federal government should allow **Christian** prayer in public schools.
- The federal government should allow the display of **Christian** symbols in public spaces.

Because we randomly assigned versions, we can compare the proportion of Americans who agreed and disagreed with each item. In two of the three cases, fewer respondents agreed with the more exclusive versions (see Figure 3). The mean shift is statistically significant, but what is perhaps most surprising is how small it is. The prayer version returns only a 5 percent drop in "strongly agreeing" with the statement. In the Christian values example, only 2 percent fewer selected "strongly agree," and 2 percent fewer selected "agree." None of the other statements showed a significant movement, including the "Christian symbols" treatment. When viewed alongside the first survey experiment, we take this as fairly strong evidence of the essential stability of the CN scale items – in our read, Americans appear to know what the questions mean (though intentions should be stated directly).

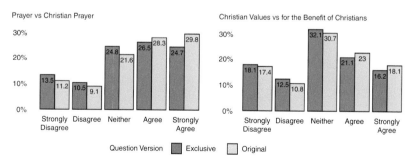

**Figure 3** Comparison of original and Christian exclusive question wording (February 2022) Note: The exclusive questions elicit less support: $p = 0.03$ for values (0.1 mean difference), $p < 0.01$ for prayer (0.18 mean difference) (*t*-tests), $p = 0.25$ for symbols (not shown; 0.04 mean difference). The treatments were effectively randomized across demographic groups.

## 2.3 A Worldview Awaiting Mobilization? Trends in Christian Nationalist Opinion

Part of our assessment of the stability of CN is to look over the long term, and we suspect that Christian nationalist views have existed within civil society for decades. Ideally, we would be able to track the expressed beliefs of elites within a portion of society that is both respected and in regular communication with the mass public (Djupe and Gilbert 2003; Guth et al. 1997; Smidt 2016). Fortunately, we can do just this.

### 2.3.1 Precursors to Mobilization #1: Elite Movement Over Time

Thanks to James Guth and colleagues we have almost ideal data from SBC clergy over a critical time span. In 1988, he began asking them if they agreed or disagreed that "The U.S. was founded as a Christian nation" and continued asking this through 2008. While the item is, of course, not a multi-item measure of CN, it is at the core of the CN scale (Davis 2022).

Figure 4 shows the shifting partisan composition of the SBC pastorate, along with their CN. By 1988, the clergy were well aligned with the GOP,

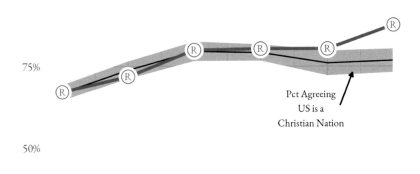

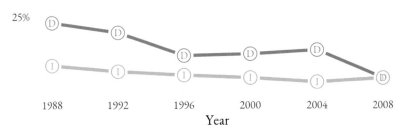

**Figure 4** Percent of SBC clergy who view the United States as a Christian nation and partisanship of SBC clergy, 1988–2008

a connection that would only strengthen with time so that by the election of Barack Obama in 2008, 88 percent were Republican – a full twenty-point increase from twenty years earlier. Likewise, in the 1980s when the SBC was wrought with internal division about control over the denomination by old guard moderates and some liberals (Ammerman 1990), the clergy already substantially agreed that the United States was aligned with Christianity. This already strong connection of SBC clergy by the 1980s – desiring the unity of church and state – would grow in the denomination as the presence of Democrats and independents atrophied. By 1996, another 10 percent agreed with the CN position, and it has remained at that level since (~80 percent).

If there was a plurality of views within the Republican Party in the 1980s, the local elites of the constituency (white evangelical Protestants) that would become its core were ready. This is not to say, of course, that talk of a Christian nation was unheard of before the 1980s. Indeed, it was common in the anti-communist politics of the post–World War II era, in school prayer controversies, and so forth (Fea 2018; Kruse 2016; McDaniel et al. 2022). The point, however, is that decades ago religious elites were leading Republicans and future Republicans through the Christian nationalist project.

### 2.3.2 Precursor to Mobilization #2: The CN Worldview in the Mass Public

For the mass public, we can track CN attitudes for a much shorter – though still informative – time span using the full CN scale. The scale was first used in 2007 in a Baylor survey, was repeated in 2017 in the Baylor Religion Survey Wave IV, and then has been included in various studies (including ours) since. Here we compress the scale to run from 0 to 1, so we interpret the shifts in the scale means in terms of percentages of the entire scale. We weighted each survey's respondents to approximate the national adult population according to the Census Bureau estimates, and the results are available in Figure 5.

The $y$ axis range is compressed to an eight-point span, so the shifts are clearly not enormous (but they do vary). The most notable change is the ramp up in CN during the Trump years to the high point in March 2020, when the adult population leaned Christian nationalist (above 0.5 on the scale). The year 2020 is also the high water mark for the use of Christian nationalist rhetoric by political elites, especially by Trump.

Christian nationalism dropped after the 2020 election and the January 6 Insurrection, but then rebounded. This pattern fits with the initial shock of many Republican elites after the Insurrection, but it is important to remember that many pivoted quickly to support Trump and embrace the so-called "Big Lie." Republican leaders also downplayed the Insurrection as "legitimate public

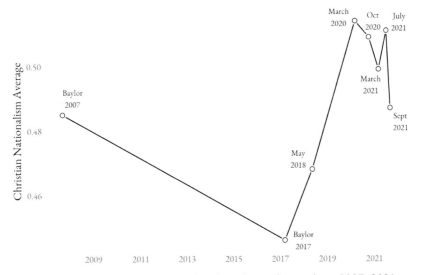

**Figure 5** How Christian nationalism has changed over time, 2007–2021

discourse," as the RNC's statement labeled it when censuring Representatives Liz Cheney and Adam Kinzinger for serving on the House Select Committee investigating the events (Weisman and Epstein 2022). The figure suggests that after midsummer 2021 CN dropped again. The shifts haven't been enormous, but they also have not been trivial. A key question is who has been moving, and when?

The party division in concentrations of CN is clear, long-lived, and stark; this suggests that the potential for mobilization has always been present (Figure 6). But, it's also worth noting that the party division does not necessarily appear to be consistent. The link with the Republican Party stands out, showing an association with the strength of identity – strong Republicans have the highest CN score within the upper clustering, while independents who lean Republican post lower ones. This pattern strongly suggests the integration of CN with the Republican Party. Independents are predictably split between Democrats and Republicans, though are closer to Democrats throughout the period.

The eye-popping trend that kicks in after 2016, however, is among Democrats. In the Trump years, Democrats adopt much more Christian nationalist worldviews, increasing by about ten points on average. Note, too, the inversion of the order within this clustering – strong Democrats post higher scores while independent, leaning Democrats consistently have the lowest CN scores. At no point do Democrats cross the 0.5 barrier, but they come close before retreating after the insurrection. It is also notable that essentially everyone drops in their CN scores in late 2021.

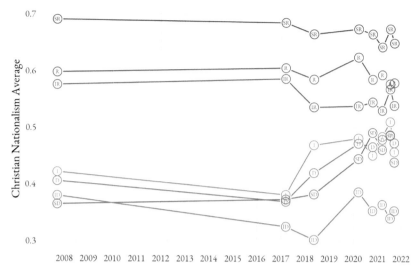

**Figure 6** The shifting Christian nationalism of the party identifiers, 2007–2021

## 2.4 Toward a View of the Missing Mobilization Story

The pattern that Democrats and Independents have become more Christian nationalist since 2016 is surely NOT what anyone would expect to see during this time period. And, it is important to keep the relative levels of CN views within these groups in perspective. Still, the patterns are consistent with the uptick in Christian persecution rhetoric that was widespread throughout the past fifteen years (i.e., during Obama's presidency, and especially during Trump's). This pattern indicates that many Democrats are cross-pressured by a CN worldview, suggesting it could be an effective strategy for Republicans and a difficult one for Democrats to counter.

It also highlights that we can't make simple assumptions about party identifiers – reducing claims to "Democrats are the party of diversity and tolerance, opposed to Christian nationalism." At the very least, we will need to assess whether CN is activated in the same way across partisan ties. The complicated relationship of CN to the parties is up next.

## 3 Christian Nationalism as Partisan Mobilization

We closed Section 2 by looking at two forerunners to mobilization – elite positions on CN and the potential for activation based on partisan breakdowns in the mass public. Twenty years of evangelical clergy data confirm that links between CN and elite positioning stretch well-back beyond the current political moment; general population surveys show that distributions of CN ideas have clear partisan signatures. Together, these findings underscore an essential point: *we must consider the role of the parties if we are to understand how Christian nationalism is shaping American politics.*

Christian nationalist views are filtered through a partisan lens as party activists seize on worldviews to advance their causes (Layman and Carsey 2002). The CN worldview may be cross-cutting to some extent, but Republican ownership makes it ripe for mobilization strategies. Salient issues that are owned by parties or candidates can be mobilized (Bélanger and Meguid 2008; Petrocik et al. 2003), and media coverage can feed perceptions of partisan ownership (Hayes 2008).

Due in part to CN's academic roots in sociology and history, partisanship has been a largely overlooked vehicle for religious nationalism in the United States. Thus, in this section we elaborate the complex relationship between partisanship and CN as we pursue the who, when, and why questions about its rise and influence.

To be clear, the significance of CN did not begin with Donald Trump. Republicans have long been Christian nationalists in greater numbers, and Christian nationalist views have become steadily integrated into the GOP as (1) the parties have become more sorted, and (2) conservative Christian activists have gained a stronger hold on the GOP (see e.g., Claassen 2015; Layman 2001). In turn, CN currents within the conservative Christian subculture have become increasingly mainstream within the Republican Party (see e.g., Stewart 2020), and conservative Christian party demanders have pushed the party to emphasize a CN worldview.

How do the parties leverage worldviews – like CN – to achieve their goals? Party activists use worldview politics to link their policy interests to the identities of their base. Christian nationalism drives partisan change and has been drawing individuals to Republican policy stances on "easy" issues (Carmines and Stimson 1989) like gay rights and gun control. A critical component of supporting such a narrative involves providing evidence that Christian nationalist effects are elite driven. Building on the clergy evidence since the 1980s, we drop additional pieces of evidence in this section. First, we show that adoption of CN is linked to deference to authority among adherents, which suggests that messages communicated are likely to be adopted (Zaller 1992). Second, we demonstrate that CN activates affective polarization differently via partisanship and that CN seems to be linked to anticipation of CP – that is, to the kinds of messages that have been commonly repeated by Trump and others. Republicans have political advantages when they emphasize CN, and the party has been increasingly emphasizing it.

## 3.1 Previous Work: Parties and Party Coalitions Provide Links between Issues and Identity

Our starting point in this story is group politics. Groups are, of course, fundamental to American politics and political parties more generally, as they help organize interests, mobilize constituents, and build political networks to win elections and govern. Arguably, the current backdrop of polarization and party sorting in the United States makes group politics an even more vital part of attempts to understand political parties. Parties are frequently conceptualized as coalitions of groups linked in an extended party network (e.g., Bawn et al. 2012; Koger et al. 2009). On a mass level, social identity theory has shown how group belonging and affinity promote partisanship and polarization (Mason and Wronski 2018). How groups are perceived to affiliate with parties is an important part of making and sustaining party identity, and can contribute to polarization (Ahler and Sood 2018; Claassen et al. 2021).

While the Republican Party has facilitated an ideological fusion of nationalism, free market capitalism, and cultural traditionalism (Grossmann and Hopkins 2016), the party also possesses strong orienting values – worldviews – which structure issue positions. Worldviews are strong predictors of political attitudes (Schwartz 2007), and these sets of political values precede and inform issue attitudes (Goren et al. 2016). Evidence indicates that worldviews are different for partisans (Graham et al. 2009), especially when it comes to "the culture wars" (Goren and Chapp 2017). Indeed, the parties have realigned around religious and cultural issues (e.g., Claassen 2015; Layman 2001), but it is important to note that the issues alone do not drive the sorting. Rather, elites have leveraged worldviews like CN to package their issue positions.

Worldviews may help link a party's ideological commitments from its activists to its identity groups. Within conservative politics, CN is just one example of such a worldview, though it is a particularly potent one – "conservation values" (e.g., preserving America's religious-political heritage) are among the most powerful in shaping preferences (Goren et al. 2016), and people respond powerfully to the threat of loss (e.g., Miller and Krosnick 2004). Worldviews and cultural values can also be used by partisan activists to mobilize their own coalition and demobilize the opposition (Leege et al. 2002), especially if the worldview – CN – is attached to a cross-partisan identity such as religion. This is what makes CN such an effective worldview to orient cultural politics on the Right.

## 3.2 Christian Nationalism Has Been Sorted into the GOP

The past half-century of American politics has seen Democrats and Republicans better align with their ideological commitments and group attachments, as Americans sort into political parties and social groups (e.g., Bishop 2009; Mason 2018). These alignments have fostered polarization among political elites, and at least some of the division within the mass public (see McCarty 2019). The political parties now offer distinct worldviews (and accompanying messaging) to mobilize their targets and demobilize opposition, with culture wars rhetoric coming to the fore (Hunter 1991; Layman 2001; Leege et al. 2002). In the process, CN has become synonymous with doing Republican politics, which puts pressure on Democratic identifiers with CN views.

As the parties have sorted ideologically and culturally, CN has clearly become the domain of the Republican Party. Certainly, CN views cut across traditional religious and political boundaries (Delehanty, Edgell, and Stewart 2018), but CN is highly concentrated among white evangelical Protestants (e.g., Jones 2016; Whitehead and Perry 2020a), a large portion of whom are Republicans. Because of this, CN's independent effects seem to be belied by their concentration among those holding conservative social and political identities, particularly as these are becoming fused (e.g., Patrikios 2013).

Figure 7 presents the distribution of a full CN index for each of the seven partisan categories in the 2007 and 2017 Baylor surveys, as well as our 2018 survey; it complements Figure 6 by showing the full range of values for various identifiers (vs. the mean values). Visually, the distributions by partisanship are effectively the same across the decade of data collection, though by 2018 the concentrations are more peaked. This is strong evidence to indicate that CN is not new, as we saw with the evangelical clergy data in the introduction. It has been present in the parties in the electorate for at least a decade and likely longer.

Figure 7 also makes clear that while partisanship is increasingly correlated with CN ($r = 0.34$, 2007 data; $r = 0.45$, 2018 data) there are counterintuitive elements out there: a nontrivial number of Independents and Democrats adopt at least some aspects of a Christian nationalist belief system.[2] At the same time, there are very few Republicans who fully reject this worldview. In this way, CN is asymmetrically distributed across partisanship – obviously skewing toward Republicanism, yet not absent

---

[2] McDaniel et al. (2022) note similar dynamics with the idea of American religious exceptionalism (i.e., that different partitions of the public buy into that idea to some degree, and not just whites, Republicans, etc.).

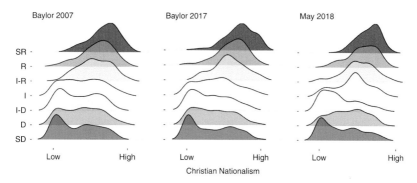

**Figure 7** The distribution of Christian nationalism among partisans

among others. This means that it is substantively meaningful to interact partisanship with CN, examining the results across the full Christian nationalist spectrum. This is especially important to do when looking at Independents and Democrats.

### 3.3 Our Expectation: Christian Nationalism Effects are Contingent on Partisanship

If CN is a partisan project, then it is worth reiterating the following: CN does not function independently of partisanship, but is conditioned by it. Most clearly, being a Republican in contemporary America is likely the equivalent to possessing a CN worldview, since the party effectively owns this approach to politics. In the same way that Republican and evangelical identities have become fused for the mass public (Patrikios 2013), the messaging from Republican officeholders and party-supportive interest groups reinforces CN and Republican ends. The connection between CN and partisanship, then, is more attuned to reenforcing social identities that bring together Christianity and Republicanism (see e.g., Margolis 2018; Mason 2018).

If we are right about the conditional relationship between CN and partisanship, what should we expect? We should see Christian nationalists sorting into the Republican Party over time. Second, as sorting progresses, an interaction term between partisanship and CN should show little to no added effect among Republicans, but larger, conservatizing effects on political attitudes among those outside the Republican Party. Third, we should see effects of CN on affective polarization contingent on party identification, ramping it up among Republican Christian nationalists while downplaying it for Democratic and independent Christian nationalists.

## 3.4 Panel Evidence Linking Christian Nationalism to Partisan Change

Figures 6 and 7 suggest that CN has become more concentrated among Republicans. However, neither of these pieces of evidence are ideal, as they come from different samples gathered via different methods. What we need is panel data so that we can assess with more confidence that CN is a driver of partisan change. Fortunately, we have that in the form of the Democracy Fund's Voter Study Group panel. Extending from 2011 to 2019, each wave included a standard measure of partisanship, which makes it ideal for this purpose. Fortunately, in a 2016 battery about American identity, the survey asked how important being a Christian is to being an American (38 percent said fairly or very important; 62 percent said not very or not at all important). While this item was not in the battery used in the Baylor study, it is conceptually close in its identification of Christianity with citizenship and belonging (for similar discussions, see Whitehead and Perry's [2020a] Appendix). It is also clear that in 2016 there was considerable variation in this belief across partisan lines. Twenty-seven percent of strong Democrats reported that being Christian is fairly or very important to being American, while 63 percent of Republicans believed the same, leaving plenty of room for people to shift their party allegiance based on this belief.

We estimated a model of 2018 partisanship with controls for 2016 partisanship, gender, education, age, modern sexism, and racial attitudes ("whether it is important to be white to be American"; 15 percent said "fairly" or "very important"). The critical test is the interaction term between a white/non-white indicator and the importance of being Christian to being an American, tapping into the linking of white and Christian identities that was mobilized by the Trump campaign (Sides et al. 2019). Race is particularly important given the lopsided partisan distributions in the respective communities. The results in Figure 8 highlight how this measure of CN appeared to drive whites toward the Republican Party early in the Trump Administration. White citizens asserting the most importance to being Christian were 0.15 points more Republican on the 7-point scale in 2018 compared to those claiming the least importance; this amounts to a 2.5 percent change. Of course, 2016 partisanship explains most of 2018 levels (as expected), but even after accounting for prior partisanship CN appears to play a role in party change, driving whites to the GOP and non-whites to the Democrats (though the latter happened more weakly, by ~0.1 points).

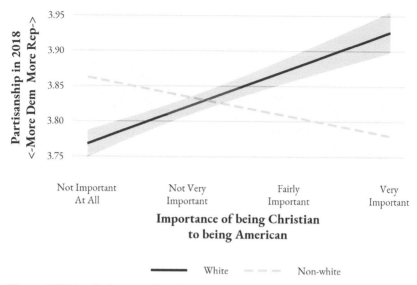

**Figure 8** White Christian nationalists became more Republican between 2016–2018

## 3.5 Policy Attitudes, CN, and Partisanship

We now look for conditional effects of CN by party with respect to positions on "easy" issues (Carmines and Stimson 1989) that have gained scholarly attention. The logic of our tests is this: over time, the effect of CN should weaken among Republicans as it is integrated into the core of the party. Leaders of and identifiers with the party adopt the worldview and its issue positions so that, eventually, being a Republican means adopting the positions of a Christian nationalist. To be more precise, we are looking for estimated slope coefficients capturing the effect of CN for Republicans that: (1) weaken over time, and (2) are distinguishable from the effects on Democrats and Independents.

### 3.5.1 "Easy" Issue #1: Gun Control

The strongest evidence that CN's effects on political attitudes are conditional on partisanship comes in the context of gun control, an issue that has been prominently linked to CN in prior scholarship (Whitehead et al. 2018). Our measures on guns are different between the 2007 Baylor data and the 2018 Qualtrics panel. To be clear, we don't think these differences undercut our results, but we want to acknowledge the difference and present the results with that caveat. In the 2007 Baylor data, 55 percent agreed that the federal government should enact stricter gun laws. In the 2018 Qualtrics Panel, fully 82 percent of the sample scored above 0.5 on our index of items – that's not surprising when fully 63 percent of the sample agrees that there should be "A nationwide ban on the sale of semi-automatic weapons." Of course, despite strong public support for gun control, the issue has been intractable in the twenty-first century, with little federal legislation passed until 2022.

In 2007, Republicans averaged 2.64 on the 1–5 scale; Independents were 0.45 points more supportive (11 percent), and Democrats 1.27 points more supportive (32 percent) of stricter gun control laws. In 2018, Independents were 0.28 more supportive (7 percent) and Democrats were 0.7 more supportive (18 percent), on average. Figure 9 shows the results from models including an interaction term between CN and three-category partisan identity (partisans include leaners). Antagonism toward gun control changes markedly with CN. In 2007, across the range of CN, gun control support dropped by 0.6 points for Republicans, and a full point for Democrats and Independents. The slopes are numerically different, but not statistically so; Republicans differ from Democrats by 0.32 ($p = 0.37$; the GOP line is less negative and flatter).

However, by 2018 Republicans drop 0.35 points in support of gun control across the full range of CN; Independents drop just over a point (1.1, 27.5 percent), while Democrats' support for gun control measures drop 1.75 points (~44 percent). By 2018 the slopes are significantly distinguishable – Republicans differ from Democrats by 1.4 points ($p < 0.01$), showing that although there is still negative movement among Republicans, the slope is considerably flatter. Looking at data collected over a decade apart, we see strong evidence that when it comes to gun control attitudes, CN's effects appear to be contingent on partisanship. Since the mid-2000s, the pull of CN

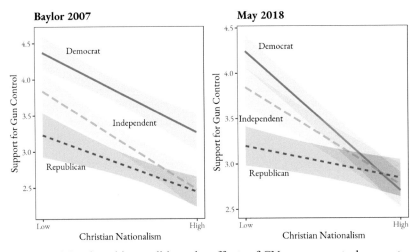

**Figure 9** Partisanship conditions the effects of CN on gun control support

has become greater for Democrats and less effectual for Republicans. This is consistent with our theoretical claim: partisanship and CN are becoming synonymous for Republicans.

### 3.5.2 "Easy" Issue #2: Gay Rights

Opinion on gay rights has changed tremendously over the past fifteen years. Entering 2007, over twenty states had banned same-sex marriage and often restricted other rights, a process Karl Rove initiated as a turnout operation for the 2004 elections (Campbell and Monson 2008). At the same time, public opinion was steadily and rapidly changing in the opposite direction, shifting in favor of granting gay rights and same-sex marriage. The landmark moment, of course, came in late June 2015 when the Supreme Court struck down bans on same-sex marriage (*Obergefell* v. *Hodges*).

Many things have changed as a result, beyond the fact that same-sex couples have gotten married across the country. The rhetoric of Christian Right groups has pivoted away from same-sex marriage to talk about "religious liberty" and abortion (Lewis 2017; Wilson and Djupe 2020) – the approach to the latter is continuing to evolve in the wake of the decision in *Dobbs* v. *Jackson Women's Health Organization* (2022). And, as more same-sex couples have pursued marriage and have planned weddings, this has brought them into conflict with conservative Christian purveyors. Such "service refusals" have gone well beyond the photographer, baker, and florist, who have made national headlines, to include tax providers, pizza shops, website builders, and others. Thus, the items we examine also cross this threshold, looking at gay marriage in a time before its affirmation via the Supreme Court, and opinion toward religious claims for service refusals, per the current climate.

The 2007 Baylor study asked about same-sex marriage. In 2007, Republicans averaged just 1.8 points on a Likert scale ("disagree"), while Independents were a point more supportive of same-sex marriage, and Democrats were 1.5 points greater in support (near "agree"). This varies dramatically, of course, based on CN (see Figure 10). Republican support falls 1.7 points (42.5 percent of the scale) across the range of CN; support drops for Democrats and Independents more steeply, and those slopes are distinguishable. Republicans' slope is 1.2 less steep ($p < 0.01$) than the slope for Democrats. In 2007, Democrats drop an astounding 2.9 points (72.5 percent) through the full range of CN, and independents are not far behind them.

Our 2018 data asked about service refusals, and the picture looks quite different. In part, of course, this is because LGBT service refusals are a different issue than approval of gay marriage. Still, we see very different

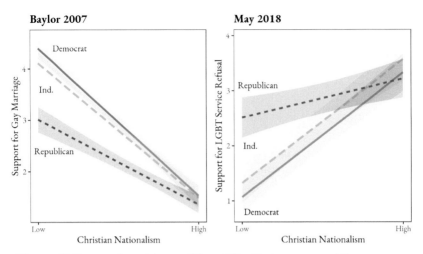

**Figure 10** How partisanship conditions CN effects on support for same-sex marriage (2007), and service refusals to LGBT clients (2018)

effects by CN and partisanship between these periods. In 2018 Republicans are just barely supportive of service refusals in these data (mean = 3.35 on a 5-point scale), while Democrats are just over a point less supportive (averaging "disagree"). However, the effects of CN have changed as the issue has evolved: Republicans are differentiable based on their CN (0.7, $p = 0.03$), though at a much lower rate than Democrats and Independents, whose support for service refusals increased by 2.25 points ($p < 0.01$) across the full range of the CN index. Put differently, in 2018 Republicans tended to take positions that looked Christian nationalist, whether they strongly adopted that worldview or not – this is consistent with the idea that the worldview has already been integrated into the party's core.

## 3.6 CN Orientations toward Elite Influence

Across a decade's span, we have demonstrated that CN is linked to multiple political attitudes, and that the links appear to be conditional and evolving with the parties. Though we do not have the ability to say that CN views are causally related to these attitudes, in this section we demonstrate that Christian nationalists are particularly disposed to react to how group interests are defined and to what group leaders have to say – after all, if CN is a worldview organized to link policy interests to a social identity, it should mean that group members are encouraged to adopt positions that maintain those boundaries.

We test for the links between CN and broad dispositions toward the in-group and in-group elites. Here we draw on national data from the 2016 Qualtrics panel study; we focus on Wave II, which had nearly 1,000 respondents. That study does not have the full CN battery, but it did ask respondents if they agreed that the United States was a Christian nation (arguably the core of the battery). Still, we would argue that any drawbacks of this single measure are offset by the inclusion of an SDO battery of four questions (e.g., Pratto et al. 1994). SDO has two components: a preference for a hierarchical social order (i.e., the idea that some groups should be on top), and a rejection of a push for equality, which could shake up the social order.

Our 2016 survey also asked about agreement with a statement that "Clergy have a great capacity to influence the opinions of congregation members," which has been used previously to document respect for religious elites. Finally, we also included a new item about (religious) elite messaging: "How important to you is what leaders of your religious group have to say about politics and current events?" The response options for these questions ranged from "not at all important" to "extremely important."

The results indicate that Christian nationalists show greater SDO (by about 10 percent, given the 0–1 scale) in the face of controls, likely believing that their place in the group hierarchy is correct. Similarly, Christian nationalists agree at a higher rate that clergy have great influence (~13 percent higher). And, they also place greater importance on what their religious leaders have to say about politics (~23 percent). These results reinforce our core interpretation about how CN works: as the ideation of in-group protection, inspired and maintained by fealty to in-group elites.

## 3.7 Affective Polarization, Partisanship, and CN: Putting the Pieces Together

Perhaps no topic has received more attention since Trump's surprise victory in 2016 than affective polarization. How does an activated Christian nationalist worldview affect the feelings Americans hold toward Republicans and Democrats using feeling thermometers? One of the primary means of activation is assertions that Christians will be persecuted under a Democratic Administration – this variable will play a starring role in Section 4. Given their partisan cast, these beliefs in forthcoming Christian persecution are likely to have varying effects when received by different partisans. Figure 11 shows this evidence (higher scores mean a greater difference in feelings toward the parties) differentiated by partisanship for both the March and October 2020 samples. The results vary somewhat across the year, but there are some general lessons.

In March 2020, there is no consistent effect of CN unless those views have been activated by CP communication via elites. For the activated, more CN

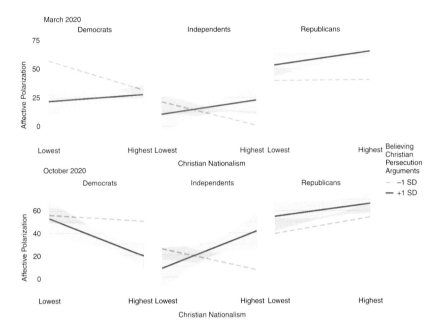

**Figure 11** How anticipation of Christian persecution is linked to affective polarization by partisanship and Christian nationalism

boosts affective polarization across partisans by about ten points. Without activation, CN is linked to less polarization among Democrats and independents, and has no effect among Republicans.

In October 2020, just before the presidential election, partisan patterns play a stronger role. Those who reject the idea of forthcoming persecution are the most polarized among Democrats and the least among Republicans. It is the opposite pattern when they do believe in CP– Democratic CNs are the least polarized, while Republicans are the most. Independents show the clearest interaction between activation and the worldview. When CN and CP work together, independents are more polarized, nearly as much as activated Christian nationalist Republicans. Cross-cutting combinations show the least polarization.

Some general lessons can be found. CN is not consistently associated with more or less polarization in itself; instead, the effects hinge on partisanship and threat. In each partisan group, persecution beliefs help differentiate among Christian nationalists. Democrats who believe in forthcoming persecution of Christians are less polarized than those who do not, further confirming that CN is a Republican project. Among Republicans and independents that relationship reverses so that persecution beliefs are linked to greater polarization. Generally, those who do not believe in forthcoming persecution are less polarized, especially when they are also Christian nationalists.

There are exceptions, of course, especially just before the general election in October of 2020. Then, Democrats who did not believe in forthcoming persecution – a major Republican talking point – were the most polarized. And, among Republicans, CN has a consistent effect driving up polarization, surely showcasing the many reinforcing claims about the dangers of Democratic "socialism," which is often equated with atheism in the American context. Republican believers in forthcoming CP are more polarized than those who do not believe.

Overall, the evidence in Figure 11 highlights the value of including activation language. Without it, the relationships look quite different – CN in both samples is linked to less polarization among Democrats, shows no effect among independents, and is linked to higher polarization among Republicans. However, accounting for threat via the activation of forthcoming persecution clearly differentiates among partisans and changes the polarization outcomes linked to CN.

## 3.8 Republicans or Christian Republicans?

The constellation of results we have presented in Sections 2 and 3 reinforces the idea that the Republican Party is now operationally a party of CN – this worldview has transformed from a niche undercurrent to a gulf stream that links and divides the two major parties in the United States. CN has long been concentrated on the Right; it is not new to the Trump era, though recent political cycles have strengthened this connection. Republicans now own CN and deploy it with great effect; it serves as a deep wedge, and even pushes independents and Democrats toward Republican positions.

Republican ownership of CN has important implications for scholars' understanding of the relationship between the Republican Party and the Christian Right. While the Christian Right has been an important part of Republican politics for at least the past forty years, the movement's success has been questioned on many occasions. Many Republican leaders in the 1980s and 1990s tried to keep the conservative Christian contingent at arm's length (Baylor 2018; Grossmann and Hopkins 2016). The early Christian Right was prone to infighting, led by a collection of small, independent organizations and lacked formal connections to the party leaders. These features hampered the group's influence and meant it had limited early legislative success. Success was largely limited to a number of cultural issues (Grossmann and Hopkins 2016), though the Christian Right did change the Party's platforms and positions of the Party's leaders, especially on abortion (Baylor 2018; Layman 2001). Indeed, some have characterized the Christian Right as being at least partially captured by the Republican Party (see Frymer 1999), with Republicans co-opting Christian Right values for electoral purposes (Leege et al. 2002). In this telling, the result of these dynamics was the Christian Right losing its distinctiveness and achieving only minimal political success.

Our findings suggest a different story. The Christian Right has succeeded in transforming the Republican Party's cultural style (Lewis 2019), making it a Christian nationalist party well outside of the long-standing pluralist, civil religious tradition the US long championed and attempted to export. Our data place CN worldviews squarely within the central support structure of the party, though it has taken decades for this pattern to firmly manifest. These results join others in suggesting that the Christian Right appears to be the party faction executing the take-over (and not vice-versa). The CN agenda has become the focus of Republican party platforms (den Dulk 2018), and conservative Christian activists possess "distinctive influence" within the party, with evangelicals being the religious group with the largest presence (Layman and Brockway 2018, 43). Rather than being captured by the Republican Party, the Christian Right has transformed the Party in important ways. The cultural style of CN is now expressed via a distinctive partisan style that may well be expressed by the label Christian Republicanism. Going forward, it is critical to examine how CN operates in conjunction with partisan identities, not independent of them.

In this way, we find that worldviews can bridge the gap between understandings of parties grounded in identity and those seeing them as collections of ideologies and interests. Christian nationalism is a worldview created around an identity, helping people connect with interests and party organizations – a linkage with participatory consequences, which we now turn to explore in more detail.

## 4 Mobilizing a Threatened Worldview into Politics

Distinctive sets of attitudes are important, but only if they accompany political action. Our argument, thus far, is that CN is not a worldview that necessarily promotes involvement on its own. Instead, the Republican Party and other conservative Christian elites have been capitalizing on this worldview to elect Republicans for several decades. That strategy, initially a Southern strategy to convert long-time white Democratic voters to the Republican Party (Maxwell and Shields 2019), evolved to an explicitly Christian strategy fully realized under Trump.

While conservative Christians have long taken on an embattled mentality that the world is allied against them, that belief took on a growing sense of urgency when Barack Obama was elected president in 2008, and especially with *Obergefell v. Hodges* (2015) legalizing same-sex marriage. That decision instantly placed them in the minority, with elites expressing all sorts of dooms-day scenarios about Christians opposing gay rights losing their religious free-dom. A group of conservative Christians filed a brief in Obergefell warning that establishing a constitutional right to same-sex marriage would silence dissent-ers and "inexorably result in additional violations of free speech rights" (Lewis 2017, 156). Justice Alito's dissent stated the Court's ruling "will be used to vilify Americans who are unwilling to assent to the new orthodoxy" (Green 2015). Trump happily stoked those fears ("Christianity is under tremendous siege" Trump quoted in Dias 2020), presenting himself as their champion. He promised in 2016 that "[O]ur Christian heritage will be cherished, protected, defended, like you've never seen before" (quoted in Scott 2017).

Surely it was more intuitive, but Trump's campaign rhetoric seemed perfectly dialed to emphasize the degree of threat posed to Christians if Biden won, as well as to ramp up the efficacy of Christian voters (that they can win). Paired with Christian nationalist beliefs that the nation is rightfully theirs, ordained by God, Trump's campaign rhetoric continued to fuel the "electoral time machine" – that is, white conservative Christians continue to shrink as a portion of the population, but their portion of the electorate has remained stable (Jones 2019). Conservative Christians are mobilizing well above their weight.

## 4.1 Christian Nationalism Links to Political Action

As a result of a determined campaign built to exploit deeply set dispositions, Christian nationalists are particularly well-positioned to engage in political action. In prior scholarship, this link between CN and political mobilization has largely been assumed. We set out to examine it empirically with three elemental forces allied to make this a reality: (1) social dominance; (2) the threat of persecution; and (3) religious involvement.

### 4.1.1 Desire for Dominance

First, the worldview of CN is itself a powerful call for Christians to lead. God ordained the United States to be a Christian nation, a "shining city on a hill" in Reagan's telling, for the world to see. As a Kenneth Copeland television show recently declared, "[W]e, the Church, are God's governing Body on the earth; ... we have been given legal power from heaven and now exercise our authority, ... [and] we are equipped and delegated by Him to destroy every attempted advance of the enemy" (Victory Channel no date). This is a powerful call for dominance that, among Christian nationalists, is a self-contained, tautological system – they believe that they were granted legal authority to rule by God, which must mean that any attempt to oppose their preferences is an act of evil that must not just be opposed, but destroyed.

The reflection of social dominance in CN seems clear through the range of research that has been produced thus far. Christian nationalism is about more than just conservatism; it is deeply concerned with Godly ordained dominance, and this is obvious when CN is deployed in politics. Yet, there has been little research analyzing how SDOs are related to Christian nationalist attitudes (but see Lewis and McDaniel forthcoming). We expect that preference for social dominance will prompt mobilization among those with Christian nationalist views.

### 4.1.2 Threat of Persecution

The previous discussion underscores the idea of a negative force to complement the positive force (God) granting Christian nationalists dominion over the United States. That is, work toward a more inclusive model of democracy is often interpreted as a rejection of God's will and therefore the work of evil forces (see Broeren and Djupe no date). Put in more familiar terms, Christian nationalists may see threat everywhere, and this is clearly linked to their desire for dominance.

Threat is one of the most powerful forces in politics (Miller and Krosnick 2004; Thrall 2007), the place where respect for rights (Petersen et al. 2011; Sullivan et al. 1982) and alternate ideas break down (Kaufmann 2004). It has, perhaps, become the dominant force in American religion and politics (Djupe 2022). One of the mechanisms that propels breakdowns in civility is that people who are high in "threat sensitivity are more susceptible to frames that invoke personal danger" (Coe et al. 2017). That is, threat sensitivity makes some people more susceptible to persuasion when linked to threat.

The United States is diversifying fast and pluralism works hard to dissolve monolithic cultures. The irony is not lost on us that the harder the Christian Right works to hold on to cultural and political power, the more it loses adherents, which generates further threat. Extreme politics (like those on display) drives people away from religious identities (Djupe, Neiheisel, and Conger 2018; Hout and Fischer 2002; Margolis 2018), in part by generating salient political controversies in congregations (Djupe and Neiheisel 2023; Djupe, Neiheisel, and Sokhey 2018).

The nature of this threat is real to the extent that people believe it. And they do. When asked what groups are the most discriminated against in the United States, white Christians say themselves, more than – remarkably – Blacks, Muslims, and others (Green 2017). Though that could be real, the fact that perceptions of discrimination against Christians are highest in the most Christian states like Mississippi strains credulity; it suggests that the belief is mobilized. In fact, in 2020 perceived discrimination seemed to go down for all groups residing among more religious nones (Djupe 2022).

This dynamic is linked to "perceived victimhood" – it's a widespread belief among Americans and is not confined to those actually facing discrimination, nor to electoral losers (e.g., Armaly and Enders 2022b; Djupe 2019). Moreover, a sense of victimhood can be mobilized; it played an important role in shaping support for the January 6th Insurrection (Armaly et al. 2022a).

As we noted, rhetoric motivating a sense of persecution among white Christians played a central role in the 2020 campaign – this was a narrative that government responses to the COVID-19 pandemic helped fuel (Lewis and Bennett 2023). Democrats were the enemy, fronting for demonic forces. Ralph Reed, an organizer responsible for the success of the Christian Coalition in the late 1980s and early 1990s, now runs another get-out-the-vote organization: Faith and Freedom Coalition. In the run up to the 2020 election, he used apocalyptic rhetoric, claiming Christians will "deserve" the persecution they receive if they don't get out the vote with sufficient vigor – it will be "open season on Christians" ( Mantyla 2019b). In Trump's words, Democrats would ban the Bible and strip Christians of their religious freedoms; Biden would "hurt God" (BBC 2020). These arguments were in wide play, such that substantial majorities reported hearing them and minorities actually believed them (Djupe and Burge 2020). In Djupe and Burge's findings, believing that Christians will be persecuted boosts support for Trump, and we find it strongly linked to CN ($r = 0.63$). This is no surprise: if the CN index is the positive embrace of the desirability of a Christian nation, the belief in CP is the fear of others clawing for their rightful position up top. Of course, the threat cannot exist without the belief in a deserved position, but the latter does not guarantee the former.

Evangelicals, for one, constantly reinforce threats in the environment – there is a part of the religious tradition that is about possessing an "embattled" mentality (Smith 1998). The broader culture presents constant temptations to Christians attempting to walk the straight and narrow. For some, this message crosses over from metaphor to reality, when Satan and demonic forces are real and walking the land, making temptations and recruiting for their evil corps. In our data, nearly 100 percent of the most ardent Christian nationalists assert that "the devil is real" and "There is evil out in the world."

Because belief in evil is high, there is an opportunity to mobilize it for political ends. And, some triggers of such beliefs are more overt than others. On a radio show, evangelical elites Franklin Graham and Eric Metaxas agreed that there was a "demonic power" working against the president (Wehner 2019).

Another argued around the same time (during the House inquiry period prior to Trump's first impeachment) that Democrats have "demons in them" (Mantyla 2019a). Even Donald Trump Jr. tried his hand at evangelical theology: "Likelihood of Nancy Pelosi praying for Trump is about the same as the likelihood of Satan running around quoting the Scriptures" (Goldiner 2020). But there are far more prosaic ways of signaling that demonic forces are about. A common refrain is that Christians need to take a stand against evil. When evangelical and Republican elites use the word "stand," it is likely that many in the audience think of Ephesians 6:11 (NIV): "Put on the full armor of God, so that you can take your stand against the devil's schemes" (see also Stewart 2022). "Stand" means much more than stand up and be counted; it's an acknowledgment of threat at the highest level, a preparation for battle against the forces of evil with God's backing. This was exemplified in Tim Alberta's reporting in *The Atlantic*, when a group called Stand Up Michigan held a partisan rally in an evangelical church to protest COVID restrictions and escalate the threats posed by the Democratic Party (Alberta 2022).

So, what is the relationship between CN and belief in CP? The data suggest a "necessary, but not sufficient" relationship. There is almost no belief in CP at low values of the CN scale, but there are some at higher levels of the CN scale who do not buy the CP story conservative elites have been stoking – they do not quite march in lockstep. Mostly, however, there is a strong, positive relationship, as we would expect.

### 4.1.3 Religious Involvement

While social dominance and perceived persecution are central features, we should not overlook other basics. Christian nationalists attend church at higher rates than those who reject the United States as a Christian nation ($r = 0.52$), even when we take out the non-religious ($r = 0.39$); this is also true within religious traditions. In the October 2020 data, evangelical CN opponents (0 on the scale) average attending "seldom" (a 2 on the attendance scale), while ardent Christian nationalists (top of the scale) average weekly+ attendance rates (a 5). That level of religious involvement, itself, even without all the threat and God-ordained seat of power ideation, has historically had powerful effects on civic engagement.

Religious involvement may have a surprisingly diverse influence on civic engagement. Per the civic voluntarism model (Verba et al. 1995), religious influence is likely to follow familiar organizational contours. That is, congregations are often filled with small groups that need to be organized and where people have discussions and build friendships. The need for organization gives members the opportunity to practice leadership, which depends on what has become known as civic skills – giving speeches, organizing meetings, and so forth. Moreover, these small groups and activities are essential sites in which social interaction takes place, and through which recruitment into politics is more likely (Djupe and Gilbert 2009). These things underscore the ways in which congregations are important beyond worship attendance.

Since involvement within a house of worship is open to all, congregations have been pitched as the great levelers, providing skills to people who may not have had access to a higher education or a white-collar job. Still, congregations do not give leadership roles to everyone. Instead, those with leadership experience – who practice such skills outside the congregation – are more likely to be chosen (Djupe and Grant 2001). It's also worth noting that congregations are not simply "vending machines" where people deposit involvement and receive all-purpose civic skills. They often impart arguments and information that guide civic activity toward particular issues or problems of importance, for example, toward protest of abortion or humane treatment of immigrants. And, they may disrupt civic involvement altogether if they impart an otherworldly worldview (Calhoun-Brown 1998) or they fail to establish the salience of politics (Djupe and Gilbert 2009). Moreover, congregations do not provide opportunities for leadership equally for men and women, with implications for their political participation (Calhoun-Brown 2010; Djupe et al. 2007; Friesen and Djupe 2017).

Those caveats aside, more religious attendance and involvement beyond worship should predict greater rates of political involvement. Thus, we expect the estimated effect of CN to fade once we control for these elements in a statistical model. Later, we will return to the question of whether congregations appear to be directing their members' political activity in a particular way.

## 4.2 Political Action Gaps

We draw on three surveys – one conducted before, one during, and one after the 2020 election – to assess whether CN is linked to higher rates of political action. Political activity can encompass a very wide range of behaviors, and we, like most researchers, asked about a subset of (seven) conventional activities: displaying a yard sign, displaying a button or sticker, working for a candidate, attending a protest or rally, contributing money to a candidate or group, contacting an elected representative, and posting a stance on social media. The mean was 1.7 activities in March 2020, which jumped to 2.0 in October, and came back down to 1.6 by September 2021; this reflects a predictable seasonality in participation (see Rosenstone and Hansen 1993).

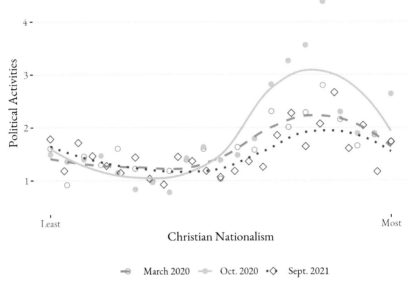

**Figure 12** Political participation across Christian nationalism for March and October 2020, September 2021

Was the October bump experienced by everyone? Figure 12 shows the average political activity rate across the entire CN scale – every value in the scale is represented and a moving average line shows the general trend. The answer is clear that only Christian nationalists experienced the October bump, with people at a select few CN scores posting considerably higher scores. This places Christian nationalists at roughly double or even triple the rate of political activity relative to non-Christian nationalists (depending on the comparison point).

The preelection and postelection periods featured more subdued levels of political activity, but still showed Christian nationalists with higher rates, averaging about two political activities compared to 1–1.5 for those scoring low on the measure. Christian nationalists are clearly showing elevated political concern, but why?

We have two ways to help sort out whether CN is primarily concerned with dominance and other matters. First, in Figure 13, we show the estimated effect of CN on political activity by itself, and then show how the estimate shrinks once we add other variables such as SDO (e.g., Pratto et al. 1994), belief that Christians are being persecuted, and the participatory benefits of religious involvement. We use data from March and October 2020 (the September 2021 results were similar to those from March 2020).

In March, going from opposed to fully supportive of CN is linked to an increase of ~1.3 political activities. However, the estimated effect shrinks as more variables are entered into the model. It barely budges with demographics, but is halved by the inclusion of religious involvement measures, and drops to the point of marginal significance when partisan strength and civic skills are entered. Here, one might say CN has negligible effects on political activity once we account for traditional explanations.

This is not quite the case in October 2020, just before the election. Then, the naive estimate of the effect of CN is sizable, boosting political activity by over three acts. Of course, the estimated effect shrinks when other measures are added. While the initial effect is cut by two-thirds, it never drops to insignificance. This accords with our story that CN was in the air in the 2020 election – a key source of rhetorical mobilization used by Republican aspirants and officeholders.

Figure 13 helps us understand that CN is correlated with orientations, motivations, and civic skills that support extraordinary political activity levels. Failing to account for these associated factors can lead to an overinterpretation of the

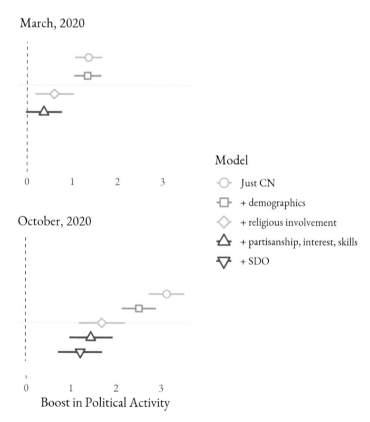

**Figure 13** Christian nationalism effects on participation are largely about other things

influence of CN itself. However, we shouldn't take the results to mean that CN is immaterial; instead, we should understand that Christian nationalists are likely to be very active because of the other associated factors they tend to possess.

But that's not the only way to understand what CN is about and how it might work to shape political activity levels. Christian nationalists are not purely concerned with social dominance or CP, and they are not all highly active in religious congregations. In the same way, non-Christian nationalists show both high and low levels on those variables. So, one key question is whether CN still augments political activity when adherents have high and low levels of those variables. For instance, would Christian nationalists still participate at high levels if they did not have a high SDO? To answer this, we can test interaction terms set in the context of the full model we have used to this point.

The results of these tests are shown in Figure 14. The upper left panel shows the interaction of CN with SDO, and reveals powerful evidence that the motive force of CN is dominance seeking. Those without a high dominance orientation

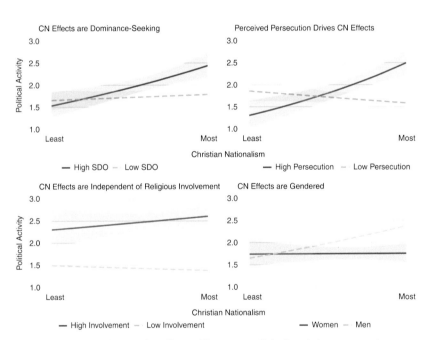

**Figure 14** Christian nationalism effects on political activity are contingent (October 2020)

**Note:** Negative binomial regression estimates. These represent four models that examined an interaction with CN individually. The model controlled for demographics, partisan strength, political interest, civic skills, religious involvement and attendance, religious tradition, SDO, and CP beliefs.

(+1 sd) participate at the same level regardless of their score on CN. But those with a high SDO score are more active in politics when they hold CN views.

That pattern also holds in the case of CP (upper right panel). There is no significant change in political activity when respondents do not believe that Christians will be persecuted, but it does increase when Christian nationalists believe that they will be. And the amount of change is about the same as it was for SDO (~a 1 activity increase). We understand SDO and persecution to be two sides of the same coin for Christian nationalists. Those obsessed with rightful dominance are constantly on the lookout for evil, unChristian forces seeking to strip them of their power and their rights. Considering that Republican elites and conservative activists were pressing both of these points explicitly reinforces the validity of these statistical patterns.

There is one explanation that does not work in tandem with CN – religious involvement (lower left panel). The results here reinforce that religious involvement does not specifically amplify the participation of CN. Instead, Christian nationalists' high rates of political activity are a result of their high rates of religious involvement, on average. They do not get more out of involvement than others who engage their congregations in the same way.

While CN does not spark more political participation over and above congregational involvement, this general relationship may be obscuring gendered effects. Prior work has shown that women do not get the same civic return on their congregational involvement (Calhoun-Brown 2010; Djupe et al. 2007; Friesen and Djupe 2017). Democratic dilemmas still apply to houses of worship, which means that leadership opportunities are often granted based on experience and stereotypes (both tend to benefit men). Since women are more religious than men, on average, congregational life could be a great equalizer to save these biases.

In the last result from Figure 14 (lower right panel), we find that Christian nationalist boosts to political activity are similarly gendered. Only men see increases in their political activity when their CN scores increase. The most interesting statement that may bear on this pattern is from Kristen Kobes du Mez in *Jesus and John Wayne* (2020). Chronicling the development of the modern Christian Right and evolution of evangelicalism, she documents the obsession with masculinity that infuses not just political issues, but also drives a patriarchal religious style.

## 4.3 Christian Nationalism Now Mobilizes Differently by Partisanship

Thus far, we have shown that (1) Christian nationalist attitudes were present among religious elites (SBC clergy) as far back as three decades ago (providing messaging/connections), (2) Christian nationalists are concentrating in the Republican Party, (3) this worldview has become effectively synonymous with stands taken by the Republican Party on "easy" issues, and (4) that followers have dispositions that reinforce elite influence. Resonance between elite rhetoric and citizen worldviews should boost the public's political engagement, not dissimilarly from the effects of attitude salience (e.g., Krosnick 1990). Moreover, the participatory boost should not be uniform, but should be conditional on partisanship, especially in the Trump era, when the rhetoric has been so overt from Republicans (e.g., Jenkins 2017).

We examined the link between CN and reported political activity across two of the datasets employed previously – the 2016 panel and the May 2018 sample (the Baylor surveys did not include any participation items). The worldview item appeared in just one wave of the 2016 panel, but there were participation batteries in each of the three waves. Each participation index was standardized; models included an interaction term between partisanship (collapsed to three categories – partisans include leaners) and CN (a single item in the 2016 panel; an index in 2018). We included controls for age, education, race, gender, income, and religious tradition.

Figure 15 displays the effect of a full shift in CN on the standardized level of political activity. The results suggest that the link between CN and participation has changed considerably across the Trump administration. In 2016, it was still a boon for Democrats to believe the United States is a Christian nation, but would not be for long. While a min to max shift in CN boosted participation by 0.3–0.4 standard deviations before the election, by early summer of 2017 Democrats were equally participatory across the range of the measure. Then, almost a year later (May 2018), Christian nationalist Democrats participated at a significantly lower rate (−0.4 sd), while Republicans headed in the opposite direction. CN Republicans were not significantly more active in September 2016 than those who didn't hold the worldview. However, since that point, CN is linked to a steadily increasing gap in activity, such that the most fervent believers engaged in almost a full standard deviation (0.9) more activism in May 2018 compared to those most opposed to CN in the Republican Party. This pattern is consistent with our arguments that worldviews are important linking mechanisms between people and political parties.

## 4.4 Christian Nationalism and Congregational Issue Engagement

When seeing 81 percent of evangelicals supporting Donald Trump (Martínez and Smith 2016), it is easy to assume congregations are reinforcing such a choice. But from at least one investigation, we get the impression that

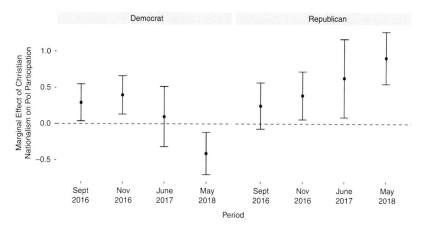

**Figure 15** CN has come to demobilize Democrats and mobilize Republicans, 2016–2018

"evangelicals were on their own in the 2016 election," without much encouragement from clergy (Djupe and Calfano 2018). It is reasonably easy to see why: Donald Trump was an incredibly polarizing figure for religious, personal, and political reasons. Clergy who made Trump salient were bound to lose members who were not already on board (Djupe et al. 2018), so the safe choice that prioritized the congregation was to avoid politics. That does not mean political engagement cannot be a reason people come to a congregation and remain a member under the right conditions (Djupe and Neiheisel 2019).

Did the safe choice prevail in the run-up to the 2020 election? Were congregations on the sidelines? One way we can assess this is by asking whether respondents heard their clergy addressing a wide variety of political issues and characters. This is not a perfect solution because of the perception problems inherent in the question – the politically interested and more religiously involved are more likely to report more clergy speech (both of which describe Christian nationalists). We include relevant controls, but wish to be upfront about other limitations: we do not know what exactly was said about these issues, and it is not easy to assume (Djupe and Calfano 2012; Djupe and Neiheisel 2008b). Also, this measure does not tell us about the amount of engagement, as single mentions and sermon series count the same. That said, since engagement is low, this measurement strategy differentiating none from some is not wholly uninformative.

Figure 16 shows that Christian nationalists were more likely to report hearing about a wide spectrum of political issues. The graph shows the difference between those at the bottom and top of the CN scale. Twenty to 30 percent

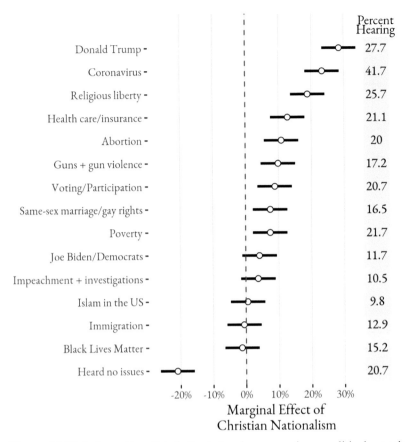

Percent Hearing

| Issue | Percent Hearing |
|---|---|
| Donald Trump | 27.7 |
| Coronavirus | 41.7 |
| Religious liberty | 25.7 |
| Health care/insurance | 21.1 |
| Abortion | 20 |
| Guns + gun violence | 17.2 |
| Voting/Participation | 20.7 |
| Same-sex marriage/gay rights | 16.5 |
| Poverty | 21.7 |
| Joe Biden/Democrats | 11.7 |
| Impeachment + investigations | 10.5 |
| Islam in the US | 9.8 |
| Immigration | 12.9 |
| Black Lives Matter | 15.2 |
| Heard no issues | 20.7 |

Marginal Effect of Christian Nationalism

**Figure 16** Christian nationalists indicate hearing more clergy political speech than others (October 2020)

more ardent Christian nationalists heard their clergy mention Trump, the coronavirus, and religious liberty. On issues including abortion, guns, health care, and voting, about 10 percent more ardent Christian nationalists heard their clergy engage. It is interesting to note that the issues concerning ethnic/racial minorities – immigration, Islam, and Black Lives Matter – were not heard more nor less often among Christian nationalists.

The far right column of Figure 16 shows the proportion of those who attend worship services reporting hearing each issue. Issue engagement is highly pluralistic and there is no issue on which a majority reported hearing about it from their clergy. The average issue was heard by a fifth of attenders. Not surprising for fall 2020, two-fifths heard clergy address the coronavirus (see Djupe and Friesen 2023). Other issues were heard by less than a third (with Trump at 28 percent, followed by religious liberty at 26 percent).

This evidence helps us reach two conclusions. First, congregations were mostly on the sidelines. While only 15 percent of attenders said they heard zero issues addressed, the median is only 2. However, the mean is 2.7, which suggests that there are a number of politically charged congregations, and further analysis shows that politically active congregations are much more likely to be attended by Christian nationalists. The top two quartiles of the CN scale make up ~50 percent of the population (of course), but they are 75 percent of the most politically engaged congregations (hearing 5+ issues from their clergy). Put more bluntly, Christian nationalists were likely hearing from their clergy at greater rates, and hearing about issues that resonated with the Trump campaign in 2020.

## 4.5 Conclusion

In this section, we have explored an uncommon model of political participation – one that places heavier emphasis on motivation. Typical models include measures of resources and mobilization (e.g., Verba et al. 1995), while their treatment of motivation tends to be closer to political interest and/or strength of partisanship (translating into a desire for "your political team" to win). That is, many prior studies have not typically identified the psychosocial mechanisms that prompt the motivation to participate in politics (e.g., Reny et al. 2019). This notion is amplified in our model, where some of the strongest elements are SDO and the belief that Christians are going to be persecuted if they do not hold onto power. Much deeper than policy disputes, these factors suggest an apocalyptic mindset, that all is lost to evil forces if the election doesn't go your way.

Christian nationalists have been participating in politics at higher rates than others who reject that worldview. Simply adopting a CN worldview, however, does not guarantee high political engagement. Instead, other factors, like SDO and persecution, are accelerants. That the pattern appears not wholly due to CN is important to know, but immaterial to the politics. Christian nationalist political ends are that much more extreme when combined with an obsession with dominance and fears of loss. When investigating CN, more attention should be paid to how it interacts with these mobilizational forces of threat and SDO.

In regard to these dimensions of political mobilization, we already know we should be concerned for American democracy when Christian nationalists appear to want to burn it down rather than cede control. That was certainly in evidence at the January 6th Insurrection, which was as "Christian Nationalist as It Gets" (Edsall 2021). But can we find such orientations beyond the narrow slice of activists who showed up to the Jericho Marches and the Capitol insurrection? That's the concern of our final empirical section.

## 5 Christian Nationalist Tensions with Democracy

"I am not talking to you. I am talking to other Jesus followers, who have power through Jesus."

– Lt. Johnny Rose, Hood County (Texas) Sheriff's
Office on the Office Facebook page

We have already mentioned that Christian nationalists have a hard time with competing ways of knowing how the world works. They do not think much of science (Baker et al. 2020a), have opposed vaccines (Whitehead and Perry 2020b), and fought back against COVID restrictions more generally (Whitehead et al. 2023). In this section, we demonstrate that they also have a democracy problem that is a result of all of what we have discussed heretofore: the mechanisms of CN as it has been mobilized into politics. That is, Christian nationalist expectations of God-granted rightful dominance in the United States, activated by claims of threatened civil liberties (posed by conservative activists), have undermined their tolerance for democracy. In the epigraph, Christian nationalist Johnny Rose is not interested in dialogue with non-Christians because "We have Power and Authority through Jesus." Non-Jesus followers are not just part of the solution, they are not a legitimate party to discussion of solutions.

Many Christian nationalists were emboldened by the Supreme Court's overturning of *Roe* v. *Wade*, not to mention the decisions in *Carson* v. *Makin* and *Kennedy v. Bremerton* – these two cases eroded the First Amendment's Establishment Clause protections while standing on guard against the persecution of religion (Lewis 2022). In the wake of *Dobbs*, prominent politicians made ending the separation between church and state (i.e., the twin protections of the establishment and free exercise clauses) an explicit campaign promise. Rep. Lauren Boebert was "tired of this separation of church and state junk." But a more thoroughly integrated example is Republican candidate for governor of Pennsylvania, Doug Mastriano, who started his campaign: "In November we are going to take our state back, my God will make it so" (qtd. in Dias 2022). Of course, his CN has been long in development – Mastriano has been a vociferous critic of COVID restrictions, has introduced legislation to ban abortion, and was a proponent of Trump's Stop the Steal gambit. Mastriano recruited alternate electors and bussed constituents to the January 6th rally: "I'm really praying that God will pour His Spirit upon Washington, D.C., like we've never seen before" (Griswold 2021).

If the Christian nationalist guiding principles are "I do what I want, and you do what I want because it is God's will," then it is easy to see how opposition would grow against decision-making procedures that are supposed to be consistent and unbiased, which describe science and democracy. Open and fair procedures enable anyone to gain control given enough evidence or votes. CN, however, is not a friend of compromise or coexistence: the idea is to promote policies/actions that marginalize and exclude political opponents, and to back procedures that enshrine CN views – and no others – into law. Underpinning what are often antidemocratic process (and policy) views and actions is a lack of respect for democratic norms. These are activated by what we explored previously: partisan attachments and perceived threat.

We are only beginning to understand the range of Christian nationalist opposition to democratic principles and processes. Some scholars have begun addressing this (see, e.g., Gorski and Perry 2022), though more needs to be done to address mechanisms. One complication is that "democracy" is near-universally seen as socially desirable, which is why autocratic regimes still maintain a gloss of democracy through show elections, and why people still think of their nation as democratic even as it backslides into authoritarianism (Levitsky and Ziblatt 2018: 20).

Of course, this is why "stop the steal" proponents framed their action as protecting democracy, because defense of democracy is refracted through partisan lenses (Goodman 2022). To take that one step further, the CN worldview can sacralize partisan "defenses" of democracy. Support for democracy in the abstract therefore becomes compromised in ways that make the response less than meaningful as an indicator of actual democratic support. Instead, it is essential to use substantive questions about support for individual rights and governmental policies and processes that describe democracy in action. In what follows, we employ this approach while looking to see how CN combines with other factors to influence support for various aspects of democracy.

There are many dimensions of fully operational democracy. Elected officials run the government; they are selected in free, fair, and frequent elections; citizens can run for office and vote in those elections (where their vote is of equal worth); citizens have access to free and diverse sources of information; citizens can criticize the government and prevailing ideas and enjoy other freedoms; and citizens can freely join organizations, including parties, religions, and other groups (Dahl 1989). Some push further to suggest that it is not enough to have institutionally guaranteed freedoms – that they must be applied and supported by a wide swath of citizenry. We start with that notion, assessing popular support for the rights and liberties of unpopular groups.

## 5.1 Political Tolerance

Support for the rights of those we dislike is essential to democracy. Elected representatives of intolerant factions may work to undermine the ability of their political opponents to express themselves, setting up elections as zero-sum games with potentially violent implications. Without rights, there is no peaceful method of dispute resolution. Along these lines, we have already discussed how conservative Christian elites have sold voters on the story that Democrats are coming for their rights. In fact, at the time of writing we were sharing tweets from former Trump administration officials suggesting, "Christians actually are being persecuted in America."[3] Expectations of intolerance (a lack of rights reciprocity – Djupe and Neiheisel 2022b; Petersen et al. 2011) raise the stakes, which supercharges mobilization and helps justify all manner of democratic norm-breaking behavior to maintain power. To reflect the importance of anticipated persecution, Djupe (2019) coined the phrase "inverted golden rule": do unto others what you expect they will do to you.

Political tolerance has been investigated as a result of three composite forces: the threat posed by a group, support for democratic norms, and various psychological dispositions like a secure personality (Sullivan et al. 1982). Religious variables have been mapped across these models, contributing to other predictors or contributing explanations themselves (for a comprehensive review, see Djupe 2015).

The belief in religious certainty leaves people with difficulty handling the diversity of views in society and undermines their tolerance (Nunn et al. 1978). This is also referred to as religious dogmatism, which some call a personality trait and others a mindset reached through involvement in a religious community (Owen et al. 1991). In either case, those with dogmatic beliefs are less tolerant than others (e.g., Jelen and Wilcox 1991; Reimer and Park 2001), even if gaps have closed over time (Schwadel and Garneau 2019).

Others examine how the social closure represented by religious involvement may undermine tolerance. In this view religious involvement is a choice to separate from the world to socialize with a more homogeneous set of people; this does not promote habits of mind pointing toward tolerance (e.g., Green et al. 1994; Smidt and Penning 1982). Of course, this line of thinking quickly runs into trouble as religious involvement is often linked to more civic engagement, and some congregations are quite diverse (e.g., Djupe and Gilbert 2009).

---

[3] https://twitter.com/William_E_Wolfe/status/1546520384270471169.

Other congregation-based explanations rely on exposure to information – explicit tolerance arguments (Djupe and Calfano 2015), relevant values presentations (Djupe and Calfano 2013), and inclusive discourse (Djupe and Neiheisel 2008b; Djupe and Calfano 2012) can all shape tolerance.

Christian nationalists already tick several boxes from the standard model of tolerance. Their religiosity is much higher than others, which may promote social closure. Christian nationalists are also more likely to adopt exclusive values – that they should associate with coreligionists ($r = 0.65$, October 2020 data). And, they are likely to be more religiously dogmatic, for instance, believing that the Bible is the literal word of God ($r = 0.52$, October 2020 data).

That said, the substance of CN should constitute the dominant link with tolerance levels. It seems self-evident that a worldview that believes the United States was founded by Christians for Christians (and should continue as such) would see the rights of others as optional or lesser. While Christian nationalists would give preference to in-group Christians, it is perhaps not automatic that they would denigrate out-groups – in-group love can move independently from out-group hate (e.g., Brewer 1999; Broeren and Djupe no date; Lewis and McDaniel forthcoming). That is, some groups may be seen as benign enough to remain coequal citizens, or perhaps threat is oriented toward in-group loss rather than out-group gain. Regardless, as we noted previously, CN has been mobilized through trumped up threats from the left, and since perceived threat is the dominant force shaping tolerance levels, we expect Christian nationalists will show higher levels of threat and lower levels of tolerance.

Figure 17 shows three looks at tolerance and the tolerance-adjacent forces of threat and reciprocity – Djupe and Neiheisel (2022b) refer to the latter as a distinctive form of threat. We also interact CN with worship attendance to test if congregations are amplifying Christian nationalist themes. Threat appears to be mobilized through the expected channels. The first panel suggests that CN is linked to feeling more threat when it is combined with higher than average church attendance (low attending individuals who are not Christian nationalists report about the same amount). The two groups that run counter to stereotype – for example, low attending Christian nationalists – report less threat.

Tolerance shows a different pattern (middle panel), though we need to remember that threat is included in this model. Net of threat, CN is linked to lower tolerance levels, but worship attendance shows a weak, positive effect, helping to buoy tolerance from sinking lower (a genuine effect here, given the interactive specification). The most tolerant, regardless of attendance, are those opposed to CN. That said, given the scores there is not much to cheer for – most

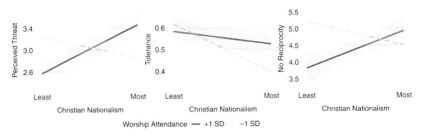

**Figure 17** Christian nationalist worship attenders feel more threatened by the other party, tolerate them equally, and expect less reciprocity (May 2018)

hover just about the 0.5 mark, which is on the fence about whether to extend rights to the evaluated group of partisans.

The last panel shows links to reciprocity – the belief that other groups would respect your rights if in power. There is one group that leans toward expecting rights reciprocity: high attending individuals who are not Christian nationalists. Everyone else, however, effectively believes that the groups they dislike will not respect their rights. In this case, attendance does not parse Christian nationalists, which is not surprising given the consistent messaging from conservative elites throughout this period. However, that messaging appears to have intensified. As a whole, Christian nationalists did not perceive less reciprocity compared to others in 2018, but they certainly did by October 2020 (about fourteen points less, which surely reflects the persecution messaging coming from Trump and others). Indeed, once we include CP in the model of reciprocity, CN has no effect – it's all due to mobilized threat.

## 5.2 Democratic Support

Many would argue that it is critical that public support for democracy go beyond rhetorical support of existing institutions – the public must reject undemocratic processes that may challenge or undermine current arrangements. Essentially, there must be a bulwark, elite or mass, that stops creeping authoritarianism. Called the "Churchill hypothesis," Rose and Mishler (1996) suggested democratic support should be measured less by its ideals and more by comparison with alternatives.

Americans have had no real points of comparison. And from one perspective, that may be a boon: democracy has consolidated and democratic support is a feature of the populace (e.g., Norris 2011). However, there are obvious reasons to be concerned about the American case (McDaniel et al. 2022) – a look around reveals an increasing number of countries (e.g., Hungary and Turkey) where well-established democracies have been backsliding without losing popular support. Frederiksen (2022: 281) discusses this, noting "as their country gains democratic experience ... they lose incentives to form opinions on the basis of threats to democracy." It is not hard to see how unanchored opinions could facilitate democratic decline when mixed with incentives that would augment the power of one's party, help pursue ideological goals, and align with elite cueing (Gidengill et al. 2021).

Christian nationalists check these boxes, and we have evidence on this point. First, 81 percent of strong Republicans and 68 percent of Republicans are in the top half of the CN scale. Though there are Christian nationalists among Democratic and independent identifiers, most are Republicans. Second, 70 percent of the most ardent Christian nationalists agree that "Moving a conservative agenda was worth any price of supporting Trump" (CN correlation with that item: $r = 0.56$). Finally, the bald-faced elite cues undermining democracy have been well-documented here and elsewhere. So, do Christian nationalists reject what we might call "undemocratic" processes? The short answer would seem to be "no" – political goals outweigh democratic commitments (see also Goodman 2022).

Figure 18 shows how Christian nationalists stand relative to others on measures of "stealth democracy" (Hibbing and Theiss-Morse 2002), which was originally conceptualized as Americans' rejection of some of the participatory elements of the democratic process, and of their support for some "nondemocratic decision-making structures" (137). We appreciate this battery's focus on process preferences, and think it's a useful approach here given its development in the American context and recent work on how individuals may "rationalize" democracy to fit their preferences (e.g., Goodman 2022). Henceforth, we discuss the results in terms of support for undemocratic processes – we think this is a fair take on the nonparticipatory and nondemocratic components of the original concept as they have entered the contemporary era of American politics.

While very few Americans – of any stripe – support rule by an "unelected, independent group of experts," Christian nationalists are more likely to support rule by successful business people, more likely to reject the idea of compromise, and more likely to urge politicians to "stop talking and just take action." To be clear, these measures are not the only measures of support for undemocratic process. And, they only minimally overlap with "undemocratic alternatives" as posed via well-known comparative data sources like the World Values Surveys. Still, these measures do offer suggestive evidence that Christian nationalists are at least open to shifts in how the American political system operates.

It's important to note that Christian nationalists' failure to reject undemocratic processes (conceptualized in this way) does not appear to be a function of the perceived underperformance of democratic institutions, at least by conventional

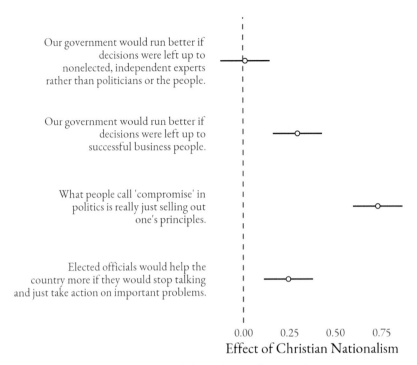

**Figure 18** Christian nationalists fail to reject undemocratic processes at greater rates (May 2018)

**Note:** Positive effects = more agreement with the statement by CNs.

measures. We also asked a number of questions borrowed from Brightline Watch that gauged perceived democratic health, including: "Government officials do not use public office for private gain" and "Government officials are legally sanctioned for misconduct" (plus four other statements; $\alpha = 0.78$). A reasonable supposition, backed by literature, is that a public giving poor performance assessments and seeing democratic institutions as illegitimate may turn to authoritarian alternatives (e.g., Evans and Whitefield 1995).

However, Christian nationalists seem to have this formulation backwards. They see American democracy as the most healthy on the scale of six items we used, but are also the most supportive of statements like "Our government would run better if decisions were left up to successful business people." At the same time, non-Christian nationalists (e.g., those with low, first quartile CN scores) also flip the usual script: they see American democracy as less healthy, but are more likely to reject undemocratic processes. Of course, it's hard not to see views of the Trump Administration in these scores: a defensiveness among Christian nationalists and a hopefulness among those opposed to CN that the

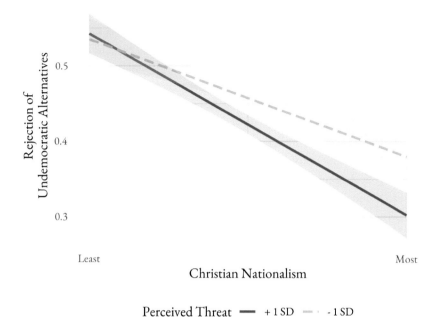

**Figure 19** Christian nationalists who feel threatened by the other party are less likely to reject undemocratic processes (May 2018)

administration of government will "return to normal" one day. To us, all this underscores how the undemocratic – and sometimes explicitly authoritarian – aspects of recent Republican politics in the United States have been driven by an elite actor rather than some abstract principle or real experience.

While we don't have the same CP measures available in our May 2018 survey, we do have measures of how threatening the other party is. What do we see? The more threatening people find the other party, the more they are unwilling to reject undemocratic processes ($r = 0.09$). And, there is an especially strong relationship on this with CN (Figure 19); threat has no such effect among those opposed to CN. Together, then, we observe that Christian nationalists are both more likely to report that the other party is threatening (Figure 17), and also more affected by this perception, further weakening their support for certain types of democratic processes.

### 5.3 "Extremism In the Pursuit of Liberty is No Vice"

We have laid out a case that mobilized Christian nationalists are intensely motivated by their in-group attachments – partisan and religious – to maintain or reacquire dominance against an array of perceived threats. It takes little imagination to suspect that they might see virtue in using extreme measures to "take America back." This isn't the first time that Christians have valorized dangerous behavior to benefit the faith. In fact, "[A]t the heart of the Christian story, the suffering of violence stands as the price of faithfulness" (Lundberg 2021). As has become common, this has been mobilized for political ends. Whether the stories of martyrs are true or inflated (Moss 2013), the myth of martyrdom may help produce new generations of culture warriors who expect persecution and accept the need for violence.

A more recent version is illustrative of conversations that have surrounded the evangelical community: the students, Cassie Bernall and Rachel Scott, killed in Columbine high school purportedly for being Christian (Wilkinson 2019). The subject of Christian pop culture (e.g., Michael Smith's "This is your time") and of multiple, best-selling books, some have noted that Bernall and Scott have inspired a generation of would-be martyrs (Cullen 2015; Rosin 1999; Wilkinson 2019).

This idea of martyrdom is important to the story of CN because rather than avoiding conflict, some conservative Christians may look for opportunities for confrontation as ways to confirm the veracity of their faith. As Alan Noble (2014) argues, evangelicals have a "Christian persecution complex" in which "Persecution has an allure," even when it is "sometimes fiction or deeply exaggerated non-fiction." The Bible itself may contribute to this mentality, with persistent warnings that Christians will be persecuted for their faith. As it is encouraged by news anchors, Christian movies (e.g., *Left Behind* ; *God's Not Dead*), and Christian bands like DC Talk, it is perhaps no surprise that some conservative Christians might come to "fetishize persecution" (Noble 2014).

Though there have long been groups in the United States that turn to violence, extreme groups went mainstream during the Trump years (O'Harrow et al. 2021; SPLC 2019). Not in the past 100 years have white supremacists been called "very fine people" by the president of the United States as they were after Charlottesville (e.g., Kessler 2020). Moreover, groups prone to violence were involved in planning the January 6th Insurrection, per the Select House Committee. Of course, one might point out that these examples are all small groups. Can we find any evidence of a broader support for violence? Is such support linked to CN and the evangelical persecution complex?

In March 2021, just two months after the insurrection, we surveyed almost 3,600 people via Lucid, drawing on items from the Activism and Radicalism Intention Scale (ARIS) – a scale focused on radicalized participation (see Moskalenko and McCauley 2009). These items asked participants whether they would support a group defending their rights under several conditions: if they sometimes broke the law, if they resorted to violence, if their rallies would turn violent, and if the police were beating members. As these items are hypothetical, we acknowledge Westwood et al.'s (2022) concerns about over-estimating Americans' support for violence. The ARIS items are distinct from those reported by Kalmoe and Mason (2022) or Pape (2021) (i.e., the items critiqued by Westwood et al.), though we would recognize the ambiguity in several of these items with respect to respondents' interpretations of what "violence" entails.

Those cautions noted, in Figure 20 we show how support for extremism is linked to CN when individuals believe more (+1 SD) versus less (−1 SD) in CP. In every case, the most ardent Christian nationalists who believe in CP are the most likely to affirm the extreme actions of groups. However, we would also note that in no case did a majority express support for these groups. Further, support among a subset – high CN/CP individuals – generally topped out in the 20–33 percent range.

What should we make of this? Two intriguing patterns emerge. The first is exemplified in the top panels: non-Christian nationalists firmly reject groups that resort to violence, while Christian nationalists are somewhat more likely to accept them, especially when they believe in CP. That is, we see some evidence

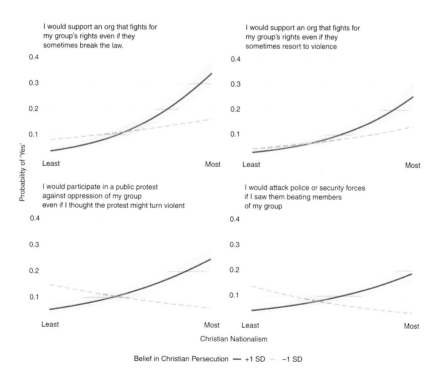

**Figure 20** Support for groups engaged in extreme behavior by CN and Christian persecution beliefs (March 2021; Logit)

that mobilized CN may be linked to support for radicalism. Still, across these ranges/combinations, the probability of supporting violence always falls well below the 0.5 mark – this suggests that actual support for violence likely remains low. The second pattern can be found in the bottom panels, and here there is some equivalence: while high CN/CP people are the most likely to support the extreme group in the questions, low CN/CP people also distinguish themselves with somewhat higher – though still fairly low – support. In contrast, high CN/low CP (as well as low CN, high CP) people are even less likely to support the extreme group (bottoming out near zero). So while there is a suggestion that CP may act as an accelerant of Christian nationalist extremism, our findings would still seem to fall in with more conservative assessments of support for violence in the mass public.

That said, the patterns related to the interaction of CN and CP are mirrored when we look at very different measures intended to gauge dispositions toward the use of violence. Using items that have appeared elsewhere (Gjelten 2021), we do find considerable support among Christian nationalists for the idea that "force" may need to be used to protect America and the traditional way of life (see Figure 21); substantial numbers also report that violence may be necessary if elected leaders can't protect America. Most critically, in the now familiar pattern, belief in CP boosts these sentiments, underscoring the potential danger of this sort of rhetoric. Without persecution beliefs, people are opposed to resorting to violence (or at least don't think it's necessary).

Perry and Whitehead (2022) argue that "January 6th May Have Been Only the First Wave of Christian Nationalist Violence." Exactly how widespread support for violence is, and exactly what some Americans see as violence may be up for debate. We also take seriously other scholars' words about being careful with the correlates of survey items gauging support for violence. Still, the consistency in the patterns of CN and CP suggest that, at a minimum, the interaction of persecution and CN views should set off some alarms and be given additional scrutiny.

## 5.4 Threat and Rhetoric Collide: The Christian Nationalist Insurrection

We introduced this Element by describing the insurrection and its dominant Christian nationalist message. Here we document the empirical links between mobilized CN and January 6th in the broader population.

The insurrection was premised on many things, but perhaps the proximate justification was to "Stop the Steal," otherwise known as the Big Lie. Trump had been trying to undermine elections since he was elected; in 2016 he claimed he

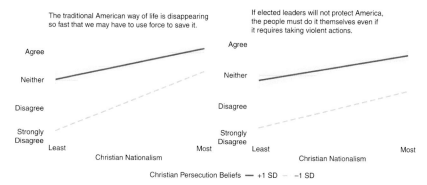

**Figure 21** Predicting other violence items from CN and Christian persecution (May 2021)

lost the popular vote because of fraudulent Democratic votes (Feldman 2020). The more egregious case followed in 2020, when Trump and his surrogates made specious claims about voter fraud that added up to a stolen election. Did his CN supporters believe him? Figure 22 suggests so – the most ardent Christian nationalists disagreed that Biden was legitimately elected and agreed that Trump lost by fraud. But their positions are far less certain than the beliefs held by CN opponents, who strongly agreed that Biden was legitimately elected and strongly disagreed that Trump lost by fraud.

Participants justified the insurrection under a broader mandate to, in the words of the so-called QAnon Shaman in the well of the Senate, "exercise our rights, to allow us to send a message to all the tyrants, the communists and the globalists that this is our nation, not theirs" (Jenkins 2021). But it's impossible to put aside that this was a partisan project that drew power from the deep insecurity that the United States was slipping away from being a Christian nation under the control of white Christian Republicans. January 6th was the perfect encapsulation of the partisan nature of mobilized CN.

So, when we look at beliefs about January 6th, it is no surprise to find that Republicans are largely aligned about the event, regardless of their level of CN. As shown in Figure 23, CN still has an effect among Republicans, but it is dwarfed by its effect among Democrats and Independents. Non-CN Democrats strongly disagreed that the "riot at the US Capitol was an effort by patriots to protect and restore our Christian nation," but CN Democrats agreed at the same level as CN Republicans. What is particularly interesting about these results is that there is more division over whataboutism. Christian nationalists strongly agree, regardless of partisanship, that Black Lives Matter is more of a threat to the United States than the insurrection. And, again, we see the same basic pattern that the effect among Democrats is twice as strong as it is among

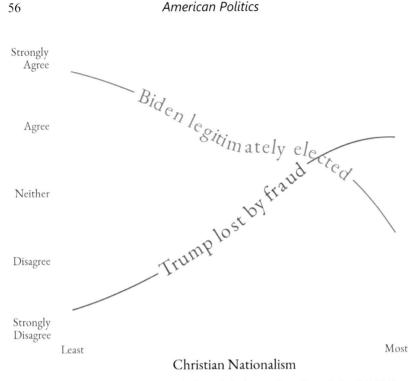

**Figure 22** Belief in the Big Lie by Christian nationalism (March 2021)

Republicans (moving four categories from the full CN scale vs. two for Republicans). To reiterate our language from Section 2, the data underscore that the Republican Party is currently a Christian nationalist party. In addition, CN is exerting a strong gravitational force on those outside the GOP.

January 6th could not have happened without a considerable amount of organization – organization we learned about from Select House Committee hearings and reports. It appears that coordination with groups like the Proud Boys and Oath Keepers was coming all the way from the top, even if most of the detailed work was handled by lawyers including Rudy Giuliani, Sidney Powell, and John Eastman (Feuer 2022; Sprunt 2022). Still, the motive force that gets Christian nationalist followers off the couch and onto the buses furnished by Doug Mastriano (Griswold 2021) is the threat of losing control of the United States. Perhaps especially in the early days after the insurrection (March), we see the confluence of CN and threat. Those with higher levels of CP beliefs were two categories (of five) higher in support of the "patriots" who stormed the Capitol. CN affects everyone's support, but support remains much lower without a fear of what a Democratic administration would unleash on Christians.

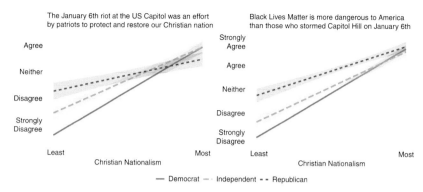

**Figure 23** Christian nationalist interpretations of January 6th by partisanship (July 2021)

## 5.5 Political Engagement of Religion among Christian Nationalists

The political engagement of religion is not illegal or unconstitutional, but it may have consequences. The more recent history of religious group engagement in politics highlights the strong reactions, both positive and negative, that people have to it. For instance, in the 1960s–1970s, mainline Protestant churches' involvement in civil rights (and against Vietnam) cost them members (Compton 2020). The 1970s also marked the rise of the "new" Christian Right that steadily made inroads into the Republican Party, though not without a fight, until white evangelicals became the dominant wing of the GOP. A particularly important year for this process was 1994, when Republicans swept into Congress after being the minority party in the House for forty years. The Christian Right was a major component of that win (Rozell and Wilcox 1995), which gave them a platform for their extremely conservative politics.

That win and visibility had consequences for religion. For one, it sparked the growth of the religious nones (Hout and Fischer 2002), whose numbers began to grow from about 5 percent to about 30 percent in 2022. But it also helped to make politics salient in congregations across the political spectrum, which exposed political fault lines, especially in states with salient political fights involving the Christian Right (Djupe, Neiheisel, and Conger 2018). Those who disagree with their congregation are more likely to leave it (Djupe and Neiheisel 2023; Djupe, Neiheisel, and Sokhey 2018), so we actually find Republicans who disagree with the Christian Right leaving their congregations. This serves to leave behind more united religious conservatives who support more strident religious involvement in politics.

The backlash to the Christian Right is real and multifaceted, with effects extending beyond the growth of the nones to include the further politicization of evangelicalism (Braunstein 2022). It is not surprising that conservative Christians are often unaware that the politicization of the faith is having broader consequences (Djupe et al. forthcoming). But this is also evolving from a point not long ago when evangelical congregations were the least politically engaged (e.g., Guth et al. 1997). As a result of this forty-year project, we expect that mobilized CN will favor a highly assertive and public role for religion.

There are several ways to show this, and we start with the role of congregations. There has long been a norm in the United States that congregations stay on the sidelines of election campaigns. That understanding was enshrined into law as the Johnson Amendment (1954) to prevent non-profits from endorsing candidates or otherwise spending a majority of their time on political campaigns (though it was almost never enforced). This norm was explicitly targeted by the Alliance Defending Freedom, which has – annually since 2008 – encouraged clergy to engage political topics during "Pulpit Freedom Sunday." Trump also discussed the Johnson Amendment on the campaign trail in 2016 as a way to cater to evangelicals. His May 2017 executive order "getting rid" of it was rated "Four Pinocchios" by the Washington Post (Rizzo 2019).

Christian nationalists are more in favor of congregations "coming out for and against candidates" – support is about 40 percent higher than among non-CNs (Figure 24). Christian nationalists are also more likely to support congregations registering people to vote, though not by as much as the previous item. Together, it is clear that Christian nationalists are not just supportive of the civil society role of churches, but of an assertive role of churches to enshrine their views in candidates and policy. Importantly, however, the perception of threat from the other party plays a significant role here as well, boosting support for endorsing candidates by 20 percent (not shown). This is the expected role of mobilized threat: encouraging groups to break long-standing norms in order to increase the chance of gaining and holding on to power.

But as would be expected by Christians who desire a nation of, by, and for Christians, their expressions of religion extend well into the public sphere. This could manifest in civil religious terms, where political and civic symbols like the flag are treated as sacred and with deep respect. But it may also extend much further. Perhaps the most striking instance of this in recent memory was the treatment of Trump himself. In the run up to the 2020 election, religious conservative public figures – for example, Rick Perry – claimed that Donald Trump was anointed by God; Perry called him "the chosen one" (see Djupe and Burge 2019). The head of Trump's Evangelical Advisory Council, Paula White, went a bit further: "To say no to President Trump would be saying no to God, and I won't do that." In May 2019, 21.4 percent of Protestants believed Trump was anointed by God to be president, as did 29 percent of evangelicals, and

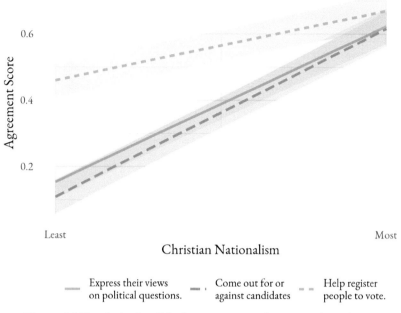

**Figure 24** The desired political engagement of congregations, by CN (May 2018)

a majority of Pentecostals (like Paula White). Belief in Trump's anointing increased considerably closer to the 2020 election (Djupe and Burge 2020; Edsall 2020).

Figure 25 shows how Christian nationalists view a wide range of religious expressions in politics. For ease of presentation, the CN scale is broken into quartiles ("4" represents the highest CN scores). Christian nationalism is linked to more of all of these beliefs, though the degree varies. We see more civil religious support for notions that burning the flag is wrong because it is sacred, though it is surprising to see such tepid support for having "In God We Trust" on currency. Although there never has been a prohibition against clergy running for office, it is not common, and there is a deep division across the CN scale on whether clergy should run: three-quarters of the most ardent Christian national-ists agree, while only 25 percent of CN opponents agree.

Other items demonstrate the full integration of Christianity with the GOP. Nearly three-quarters of strong Christian nationalists believed in October 2020 that Trump was anointed by God to be president, so it is no surprise to see the same number say the "bond is healthy and lasting" between the GOP and Christianity. We get a sense that this connection is seen as ideological, as

**Figure 25** Christian nationalists are more likely to break norms about the political engagement of religion (October 2020)

about 70 percent believe that moving a conservative agenda was worth any price. Fewer, though still a majority, agree with Ralph Reed's quip that Christians deserve the persecution they will get (from Democrats) if they fail to get out the vote at high enough rates to win. The general pattern fits with recent research finding CN is distinct from measures of civil religion – CN is more strongly tied to Republican identity than measures of civil religion, though the two move in the same direction (Vegter et al. 2023).

Of course, we cannot forget the mobilizing role of threat in pushing norm-breaking beliefs. Figure 26 shows that believing that Trump was anointed by God to be president is quite strongly linked to believing in CP. To be clear, we can't be sure if this link is causal – both were arguments conveyed by conservative elites, often at the same time. That is, the reason that Trump was anointed by God, in common telling, is that he was given a special role to protect

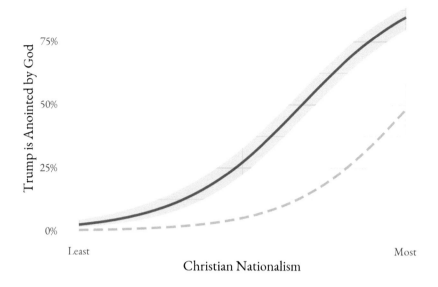

**Figure 26** The role of persecution beliefs in mobilizing the anointing of trump (October 2020; Logit)

Christians. Many compared him to the biblical Persian King Cyrus, who was not a Christian or a Jew, but allowed Jewish exiles to return and rebuild the temple (Block 2018). Given that context, it is at least logical to think that persecution beliefs are propelling such ideas as Trump's anointing.

## 5.6 Conclusion

In March 2021, long-time world democracy observer, Freedom House, downgraded democracy in the United States to reside alongside flawed democracies such as those in Romania, Croatia, and Panama (Freedom House 2021). The report cites racial inequalities, special interest influence, and polarization. Lest we think this was a one-off, the Swedish Institute for Democracy and Electoral Assistance also noted democratic backsliding in the United States beginning in 2016 (Navarre 2021). Though the rankings take in different criteria, there is widespread agreement that democracy is threatened in the United States.

Assigning blame is complex in such a diverse country as the United States, and that is not our aim in this study. Some observers have pinpointed CN attitudes in isolation. We would emphasize that mobilized CN integrates strong partisan commitments and heightened perception of threats, which allow it to be a conduit for partisan aims to rule from a minority position. Two of the three most recent Republican administrations did not win the popular vote, and Senate Republican majorities do not have the support of a majority of voters in the United States with the chamber's bias toward small states. Given their disadvantaged position, the Republican Party needs to convince their supporters to vote at high rates, which necessitates threat. And, the language used to threaten has gotten more extreme, even encompassing notions like demonic possession (e.g., Kilgore 2019) – that is, anything that highlights the dangers of allowing Democrats to control the federal government.

Once Democrats are seen as backed by evil forces bent on the persecution of Christians, the likelihood that "anything goes" increases. This is the central concern: Democrats do not deserve access to Constitutional liberties because you have been led to expect Democrats not to uphold yours – "do unto others as you expect they would do unto you." We can debate how much support there is for violent action (it is certainly >0), but many Christian nationalists support the January 6ers who took action in the names of Jesus and Trump. Perceived threat is the crucial piece that connects Christian nationalist opposition to institutions and groups that would stand in their way.

In this section's epigraph, Lt. Rose said, "I'm not talking to you," only to the Jesus followers who have "Power and Authority." In its full expression, strong Christian nationalists favor a style of politics where Christianity is fully integrated and forthright – where Republicans stand with the full armor of God, and where Republicans losing means the electorate is acting against God and must be stopped. Obviously, there aren't any scenarios in a diverse nation such as the United States – or any other nation for that matter – where such a dynamic would go well. We turn to discuss the future of CN, the major parties, and of democratic practice in the United States in our final, concluding section.

## 6 Conclusion: Putting Christian Nationalism in Context

On June 24, 2022, the conservative majority on the Supreme Court struck down *Roe* v. *Wade* in *Dobbs* v. *Jackson Women's Health Organization*. In its wake, commentator Katherine Stewart (2022) noted that "Christian Nationalists Are Excited About What Comes Next." CN politicians have been pushing measures in states to outlaw abortion without exception and criminalize women seeking abortions; some leaders of the antiabortion movement have stepped up arguments for a national ban, establishing the personhood rights of the fetus. Armed with the arguments from Justice Clarence Thomas's concurrence, Stewart described "substantive due process" rulings that might be in jeopardy, including the right to contraceptives and LGBTQ rights, though federal legislation signed into law in December 2022 protects same-sex marriage.

Extreme views seem to have become more mainstream, but they are not new to those who have studied religion and politics for some time. Elements of the Christian Right have long integrated CN with extreme positions against abortion and gay and lesbian rights. From the Fundamentalists to Jerry Falwell, and the Christian Coalition to Ted Cruz, elites have fused support for Christian America with the fear of the godless left. What has changed is how these views have been mobilized in American politics, and their ascendance within the Republican Party – indeed, the question we might ask ourselves about abortion is why did *Dobbs* happen now? What constellation of factors led to new discourse on the issue and overturning fifty years of legal precedent?

Similarly, our goal in this Element has been to put CN in context by refocusing on how, why, and when questions. That is, we have argued forcefully that to understand the role of CN in American politics we must pay attention to more than the connection between the CN worldview and snapshots of public policy attitudes. This is why we focused our Element on the 3 Ms: measurement, mechanisms, and mobilization.

## 6.1 To Recap: The Questions We Should Be Asking

Measurement: We need to be clear about what CN is, we need to scrutinize the bounds of the concept, and we need to recognize its presence in the political ecosystem over a longer time horizon.

Mechanisms: We need to understand how Christian nationalist opinion is formed in the public and how those mechanisms are linked to support for policies and parties, leveraging what we know about threat and dispositions like SDOs.

Mobilization: We need to understand how opportunistic leaders, especially within political parties, leverage these opinion mechanisms, especially threat, to mobilize CN into action.

## 6.2 Summary: Our Answers to These Questions

Measurement: We find that, while improvements can be made, well-known measures of CN seem to be capturing a stable worldview that is indeed Christian exclusive. This worldview has long been supported by religious elites (our evidence stretches back to the 1980s) – this is consistent with the idea of elite movement preceding mass public movement. We see the potential for partisan mobilization by the late 2000s, with CN ideas resonating with self-identified Republicans at considerably higher rates.

Mechanisms: We explore how CN views are formed and advanced. This suggests that we must focus on understanding which individuals are more likely to support CN, who are more likely to perceive threat (CP), who have dispositions that jell with a zero-sum worldview like CN, and who hears messaging from elites. We document all of these mechanisms, as well as their overlaps with Republican party identification and their interplays with one another.

Mobilization: We demonstrate how patterns of latent support for CN are activated by elite rhetoric, particularly among those with certain predispositions. CN mobilization has consequences for both opinion and action.

## 6.3 The Work That Remains

Looking across the sweeping coverage and rapidly growing body of work on CN, it may seem like there is little left to be done. However, we believe that this research agenda is only in its infancy. We note three main areas – dovetailing with our 3 Ms framework – that should be addressed by future scholarship.

### 6.3.1 On Measurement

Debates will and should continue about the degree to which CN is a stable disposition, and about how it differs from related concepts like American religious exceptionalism (McDaniel et al. 2022). From our time series in Section 2, it seems clear that CN has shifted consistently with a Christian nationalist surge during the Trump years. We do not have access to panel data that tracks individual CN over time, so we cannot say definitively what the dynamics are – that is, who shifted and why. Figure 27 shows that there was a dramatic surge in the third quartile of the measure (0.5–0.749 CN scores) in the Trump era; this was accompanied by dips in the first and second quartiles. The rates of what we can safely call the most ardent CNs (those in the fourth quartile –"4s") have remained relatively stable across this period. A number of forces could account for this, but we suspect that CN became socially acceptable through elite rhetoric about threat and the rightfulness of Christian power.

In our experiments, we did not see CN budge much: we found that despite apparent ambiguities in the question wording, Americans appear to understand the exclusive intent of the questions (though more explicitly exclusive wording does draw down support somewhat). The exception is in Section 3, where we show that Republicans respond to priming minority status by expressing somewhat lower Christian nationalist scores. Though they are not the same treatments, what we find conflicts with the evidence from Al-Kire et al. (2021), who show that priming religious demographic change (just a year earlier in 2019)

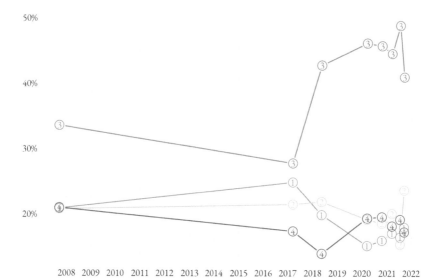

**Figure 27** Shifts in Christian Nationalism Quartiles, 2007–2021

leads Christians to higher levels of conservatism, CN, and support for Trump. At stake is a critical question for future American politics: are Republicans just on the CN bandwagon while it is winning, or are such beliefs heartfelt and enduring?

### 6.3.2 On Mechanisms

We have shown that messages – focused on threat/persecution – delivered through political and organizational channels develop and activate CN, particularly among those high in SDO. But can these delivery mechanisms be intercepted or repurposed? Initiatives and organizations have formed in order to provide resources to congregations to combat CN. There is limited evidence yet whether and to what extent these efforts might chip away at the conflation of religious and political identities, though there are studies in the works that follow some of these lines of argument. We have doubts that these efforts will achieve much, because we suspect that participating clergy would involve their congregations when they already feature opposition to CN – that is, we are concerned about self-selection. Those with divided congregations stand to lose a considerable amount by taking CN head on (as the experience of the mainline in the 1960s regarding civil rights demonstrates).

Further, on the point of congregations as settings for activation, we would also emphasize a methodological note regarding attendance – that is, the most common way that we gauge religious behavior in the United States. Scholars need to exercise caution when using and interpreting such measures in models with CN: highly correlated variables can behave strangely in regression models. As Djupe, Friesen, et al. (no date) show, controlling for CN often encourages "suppression effects" on worship attendance, so that attendance may sometimes flip its sign from a conservative to a liberal relationship. This statistical artifact is incredibly common in this literature, though one that only a few papers discuss.

### 6.3.3 On Mobilization

We have focused on telling the story of CN as a partisan project. And, in doing so, we have conditioned on the usual demographic characteristics. However, another debate that lurks within the literature is the degree to which CN dynamics are largely owned by white Christians. On the face of it – Donald Trump's in particular – whiteness would seem to be controlling (Perry and Whitehead 2015, 2021; Perry, Whitehead, and Davis 2019), especially given the tight connection of racial hostility with the Republican Party (e.g., Shaffner 2022).

Some tantalizing evidence from a forthcoming book from Michael Emerson and Glenn Bracey also suggests the power of white identity; they argue that many whites are not Christians at all, but belong to a religion of whiteness (Emerson 2022). However, we are curious about policy issues that are not racialized. Many of the relationships we present in this volume show consistent effects of CN by racial groups, though we did not have the space to demonstrate that. And the Baylor CN measure has roughly equal average scores among Blacks, Hispanics, and whites in our various datasets.

Still, there is considerable research to be done to assess the points at which CN effects diverge among white and non-white Christians. In particular, we think the approach taken by McDaniel, Nooruddin, and Shortle (2022) in their analysis of ARE is one that other scholars should follow – rather than limiting ourselves to the inclusion of indicator variables in regressions, scholars should prioritize the collection of oversamples of minority respondents (e.g., their 2012 RWS Study) so that within and between questions can receive equal consideration. And, as McDaniel et al. also note, the historical experiences of racial and ethnic groups need to be examined if we're going to understand contemporary religious-political dynamics. Incorporating history is an important part of the process of placing things in context, and this is certainly true when studying Black, Latino/a, and other non-white Americans' relationships with CN in the United States. Additionally, more work must be done to empirically test the role of whiteness in CN, especially if scholars are going to start referring to the concept as White CN (e.g., Gorski and Perry 2022). As it stands, race is not explicit in the CN index, and showing the effects among whites does not establish that race is central to its construction.

Also on the issue of mobilization, there is continued debate about whether CN is actually religious and has roots sunk in American congregations. Of course there is a theological debate about whether the conflation of a national identity with a Christian one is idolatry, but we mean something different. While we can point to specific churches that further this worldview (e.g., Robert Jeffress' First Baptist), we do not have systematic evidence about how extensive Christian nationalist behavior, rhetoric, and symbols are in American congregations (aside from the SBC clergy data we analyzed), or other organizational settings (particularly those affiliated with the GOP). Scholars need to invest time and resources gathering measures of exposure to Christian nationalist symbols and rhetoric.

## 6.4 Can a Citizenry Dressed in the Armor of God Practice Democracy?

The optimistic read of the 2020 election was that CN was on its way out with Trump's loss and the discrediting events of January 6th, 2021. And, we found some evidence that CN levels came down from their Spring to Summer 2020 peak. It's important to note, however, that much of the decline appeared to be from Democrats, with somewhat less from Republicans. Of course, this is much of our story about CN: it is a partisan project that is also pulling conservatives from the Democratic Party in the hopes of either demobilizing them or activating them to benefit Republicans. Christian nationalists of all partisan stripes take more conservative positions on most issues. Moreover, effects appear to be weaker among Republicans and stronger among Democrats, which is what we would expect to see as the GOP has long been taking CN stands. The result of this well-established mobilization of CN is that diversity among Republicans is declining; this may make the GOP a smaller party, but also one that is incredibly effective.

It would be a mistake to suggest that the GOP – which we have demonstrated can fairly be called a party of CN – is solely interested in ideological goals. After all, we wouldn't say this about the Democratic Party either. Still, the evidence presented would suggest that the CN project is uniquely uninterested in coexistence or compromise. Rather, dominance would appear to be closer to the core concern, and thus Christian nationalists seem to show less support for decision-making processes that could result in them sharing or ceding control. Science involves such processes, as of course does democracy. If the United States is of, by, and for Christians, then steps must be taken to safeguard institutions from control by others.

Thus, activated CN would seem to be one of the more dangerous threats to American democracy today (see also Onishi 2023). The claims to rightful power by a minority of Americans espousing highly exclusive notions of citizenship and rights make democratic politics extraordinarily difficult, perhaps impossible. American Christianity was not always this way, but Christianity's fall from clear and uncontested majority status has had serious consequences for politics. Christian nationalist rhetoric is now a conversation stopper (Rorty 1994): when "my God will make it so" is a campaign speech, there is little to say to the other side, or even to non-"Jesus followers" of the same party. Furthermore, if the only rightful authority is God, then steps taken to ensure minority Christian rule would appear not only legitimate and imperative, but would be rationalized as democratic in nature (Goodman 2022). Can American democracy survive – let alone work well – under these strains? We suspect the answer is yes, though it will involve elites urging their armies to lower their swords and shields.

# References

Achen, Christopher H. 2002. "Toward a New Political Methodology: Microfoundations and ART." *Annual Review of Political Science* 5: 423–450.

Ahler, Douglas J., and Gaurav Sood. 2018. "The Parties in Our Heads: Misperceptions about Party Composition and Their Consequences." *The Journal of Politics* 80(3): 964–981.

Al-Kire, Rosemary L., Michael H-. Pasek, Jo-Ann Tsang, and Wade C. Rowatt. 2021. "Christian No More: Christian Americans are Threatened by Their Impending Minority Status." *Journal of Experimental Social Psychology* 97, 104223.

Alberta, Tim. 2022. "How Politics Poisoned the Evangelical Church." *The Atlantic*. May 10. www.theatlantic.com/magazine/archive/2022/06/evangelical-church-pastors-political-radicalization/629631/. Accessed January 15, 2023.

Ammerman, Nancy T. 1990. *Baptist Battles: Social Change and Religious Conflict in the Southern Baptist Convention*. New Brunswick, NJ: Rutgers.

Armaly, Miles T., David T. Buckley, and Adam M. Enders. 2022a. "Christian Nationalism and Political Violence: Victimhood, Racial Identity, Conspiracy, and Support for the Capitol Attacks." *Political Behavior* 44: 937–960.

Armaly, Miles T., and Adam M. Enders. 2022b. "'Why Me?' The Role of Perceived Victimhood in American Politics." *Political Behavior* 44, 1583–1609. https://doi.org/10.1007/s11109-020-09662-x.

Baker, Joseph O., Samuel L. Perry, and Andrew L. Whitehead. 2020a. "Keep America Christian (and White): Christian Nationalism, Fear of Ethnoracial Outsiders, and Intention to Vote for Donald Trump in the 2020 Presidential Election." *Sociology of Religion* 81(3): 272–293.

Baker, Joseph O., Samuel L. Perry, and Andrew L. Whitehead. 2020b. "Crusading for Moral Authority: Christian Nationalism and Opposition to Science." *Sociological Forum* 35(3): 587–607.

Bawn, Kathy, Marty Cohen, David Karol, Seth Masket, Hans Noel, and John R. Zaller. 2012. "A Theory of Political Parties: Groups, Policy Demands and Nominations in American Politics." *Perspectives on Politics* 10(3): 571–597.

Baylor, Christopher. 2018. *First to the Party: The Group Origins of Party Transformation*. Philadelphia, PA: University of Pennsylvania Press.

BBC. 2020. "US Election 2020: Trump Says Opponent Biden Will 'Hurt God'." August 7. www.bbc.com/news/election-us-2020-53688009. Accessed September 2, 2022.

Bélanger, Éric, and Bonnie M. Meguid. 2008. "Issue Salience, Issue Ownership, and Issue-Based Vote Choice." *Electoral Studies* 27(3): 477–491.

Bellah, Robert N. 1967. "Civil Religion in America." *Daedalus* 96(1): 1–21.

Bellah, Robert N., and Phillip E. Hammond. 2013. *Varieties of Civil Religion*. Eugene, OR: Wipf and Stock.

Bishop, Bill. 2009. *The Big Sort: Why the Clustering of Like-Minded America Is Tearing Us Apart*. New York: Houghton Mifflin.

Block, Daniel. 2018. "Is Trump Our Cyrus? The Old Testament Case for Yes and No." *Christianity Today.* October 29. www.christianitytoday.com/ct/2018/october-web-only/donald-trump-cyrus-prophecy-old-testament.html. Accessed July 16, 2022.

Boorstein, Michelle. 2021. "A Horn-Wearing 'Shaman.' A Coyboy Evangelist. For some, the Capitol Attack Was a Kind of Christian Revolt." *The Washington Post.* July 6. www.washingtonpost.com/religion/2021/07/06/capitol-insurrection-trump-christian-nationalism-shaman/.

Braunstein, Ruth. 2022. "A Theory of Political Backlash: Assessing the Religious Right's Effects on the Religious Field." *Sociology of Religion* 83 (3): 293–323.

Brewer, Marilyn B. 1999. "The Psychology of Prejudice: Ingroup Love and Outgroup Hate?" *Journal of Social Issues* 55(3): 429–444.

Broeren, Zachary D., and Paul A. Djupe. No date. "The Ingroup Love and Outgroup Hate of Christian Nationalism: Experimental Evidence about the Rule of Law." Unpublished manuscript.

Burge, Ryan P. 2021. "Why 'Evangelical' Is Becoming Another Word for 'Republican'". *The New York Times.* October 26. www.nytimes.com/2021/10/26/opinion/evangelical-republican.html. Accessed January 15, 2023.

Calhoun-Brown, Allison. 1998. "While Marching to Zion: Otherworldliness and Racial Empowerment in the Black Community." *Journal for the Scientific Study of Religion* 37(3): 427–439.

Calhoun-Brown, Allison. 2010. "This Far by Faith: Religion, Gender, and Efficacy." In *Religion and Democracy in the United States: Danger or Opportunity*, Alan Wolfe and Ira Katznelson, eds., 279–307. New York: Russell Sage.

Campbell, David E., and J. Quin Monson. 2008. "The Religion Card: Gay Marriage and the 2004 Presidential Election." *Public Opinion Quarterly* 72 (3): 399–419.

Carmines, Edward G., and James A. Stimson. 1989. *Issue Evolution: Race and the Transformation of American Politics*. Princeton, NJ: Princeton University Press.

Claassen, Ryan L. 2015. *Godless Democrats and Pious Republicans?* New York: Cambridge.

Claassen, Ryan L., Paul A. Djupe, Andrew R. Lewis, and Jacob R. Neiheisel. 2021. "Which Party Represents My Group? The Group Foundations of Partisan Choice and Polarization." *Political Behavior* 43: 615–636.

Coe, Chelsea M., Kayla S. Canelo, Kau Vue, Matthew V. Hibbing, and Stephen P. Nicholson. 2017. "The Physiology of Framing Effects: Threat Sensitivity and the Persuasiveness of Political Arguments." *Journal of Politics* 79(4): 1465–1468.

Compton, John W. 2020. *The End of Empathy: Why White Protestants Stopped Loving Their Neighbors*. New York: Oxford University Press.

C-SPAN. 2022. "User Clip: Paula White Jan 6 Prayer." January 3. www.c-span.org/video/?c4993902/user-clip-paula-white-jan-6-prayer. Accessed January 15, 2023.

Cullen, Dave. 2015. "Why Does the Columbine Myth about 'Martyr' Cassie Bernall Persist?" https://newrepublic.com/article/122832/why-does-columbine-myth-about-martyr-cassie-bernall-persist. Accessed July 5, 2022.

Dahl, Robert A. 1989. *Democracy and Its Critics*. New Haven, CT: Yale University Press.

Davis, Nicholas T. 2022. "The Psychometric Properties of the Christian Nationalist Scale." *Politics and Religion* 16(1): 1–26. https://doi.org/10.1017/S1755048322000256.

Davis, Susan. 2022. "Trump Speaks to Faith and Freedom Coalition as Jan. 6 Hearings Continue." *NPR*. June 17. www.npr.org/2022/06/17/1105970790/trump-speaks-to-faith-and-freedom-coalition-as-jan-6-hearings-continue. Accessed January 15, 2023.

Delehanty, Jack, Penny Edgell, and Evan Stewart. 2018. "Christian America? Secularized Evangelical Discourse and the Boundaries of National Belonging." *Social Forces* 97(3): 1283–1306.

den Dulk, Kevin. 2018. "The GOP, Evangelical Elites, and the Challenge of Pluralism." In *The Evangelical Crackup? The Future of the Evangelical-Republican Coalition*, Paul A. Djupe and Ryan L. Claassen, eds. 63–76. Philadelphia, PA: Temple University Press.

Dias, Elizabeth. 2020. "'Christianity Will Have Power'." New York Times. August 9. www.nytimes.com/2020/08/09/us/evangelicals-trump-christianity.html. Accessed July 5, 2022.

Dias, Elizabeth. 2022. "The Far-Right Christian Quest for Power: 'We are Seeing Them Emboldened'." *New York Times*. July 13. www.nytimes.com/2022/07/08/us/christian-nationalism-politicians.html. Accessed July 10, 2022.

Djupe, Paul A., ed. 2015. *Religion and Political Tolerance in America: Advances in the State of the Art*. Philadelphia, PA: Temple University Press.

Djupe, Paul A. 2019. "The Inverted Golden Rule: Are Atheists as Intolerant as Evangelicals Think They Are?" *Religion in Public*. December 23. https://religioninpublic.blog/2019/12/23/the-inverted-golden-rule-are-atheists-as-intolerant-as-evangelicals-think-they-are/. Accessed July 12, 2022.

Djupe, Paul A. 2022. "The Religious Politics of Threat in Religion and Politics Research." In *Handbook of Politics & Public Opinion*, Thomas J. Rudolph, ed. Northampton, MA: Edward Elgar.

Djupe, Paul A. Forthcoming. "And They Shall Know Me by Your Trump Support: The Political Sociology of Politicized Religion." In *Trump and the Transformation of Religion and Politics*, Anand E. Sokhey and Paul A. Djupe, eds. Philadelphia: University of Pennsylvania Press.

Djupe, Paul A., and Ryan P. Burge. 2019. "Was Donald Trump Anointed by God? Are All Presidents Anointed by God?" *Religion in Public*. November 25. https://religioninpublic.blog/2019/11/25/was-donald-trump-anointed-by-god-are-all-presidents-anointed-by-god/. Accessed July 15, 2022.

Djupe, Paul A., and Ryan P. Burge. 2020. "Trump the Anointed." Religion in Public. May 11. https://religioninpublic.blog/2020/05/11/trump-the-anointed/. Accessed July 15, 2022.

Djupe, Paul A., and Brian R. Calfano. 2012. "The Deliberative Pulpit: The Democratic Norms and Practices of the PCUSA." *Journal for the Scientific Study of Religion* 51(1): 90–109.

Djupe, Paul A., and Brian R. Calfano. 2013. "Religious Value Priming, Threat, and Political Tolerance." *Political Research Quarterly* 66(4): 767–779.

Djupe, Paul A., and Brian R. Calfano. 2015. "The Golden Rule Theory: The Nature of Clergy Influence on Congregational Political Tolerance." In *Religion and Political Tolerance in America: Advances in the State of the Art*, Paul A. Djupe, ed., 34–50. Philadelphia. PA: Temple University Press.

Djupe, Paul A., and Brian R. Calfano. 2018. "Evangelicals Were on Their Own in the 2016 Elections." In *The Evangelical Crackup? The Future of the Evangelical-Republican Coalition*. Paul A. Djupe and Ryan L. Claassen, eds., 15–31. Philadelphia, PA: Temple University Press.

Djupe, Paul A., and Amanda J. Friesen, eds. 2023. *'An Epidemic Among My People:' Religion, Politics, and COVID-19 in the United States.* Philadelphia, PA: Temple University Press.

Djupe, Paul A., Amanda Friesen, Andrew R. Lewis, Anand E. Sokhey, Ryan P. Burge, and Zach Broeren. No date. "Attending Church Encourages Acceptance of Atheists: A Note on Suppression Effects in Religion and Politics Research." Unpublished manuscript.

Djupe, Paul A., and Christopher P. Gilbert. 2003. *The Prophetic Pulpit: Clergy, Churches, and Communities in American Politics*. Lanham, MD: Rowman & Littlefield.

Djupe, Paul A., and Christopher P. Gilbert. 2009. *The Political Influence of Churches*. New York: Cambridge University Press.

Djupe, Paul A., and J. Tobin Grant. 2001. "Religious Institutions and Political Participation in America." *Journal for the Scientific Study of Religion* 40(2): 303–314.

Djupe, Paul A., and Jacob R. Neiheisel. 2008a. "Christian Right Horticulture: Grassroots Support in a Republican Primary Campaign." *Politics & Religion* 1(1): 55–84.

Djupe, Paul A., and Jacob R. Neiheisel. 2008b. "Clergy Deliberation on Gay Rights and Homosexuality." *Polity* 40(4): 411–435.

Djupe, Paul A., and Jacob R. Neiheisel. 2019. "Political Mobilization in American Congregations: A Test of the Religious Economies Perspective." *Politics & Religion* 12(1): 123–152.

Djupe, Paul A., and Jacob R. Neiheisel. 2022a. "The Religious Communication Approach and Political Behavior." *Advances in Political Psychology* 43(S1): 165–194.

Djupe, Paul A., and Jacob R. Neiheisel. 2022b. "The Dimensions and Effects of Reciprocity in Political Tolerance Judgments." *Political Behavior* 44: 895–914.

Djupe, Paul A., and Jacob R. Neiheisel. 2023. "Are Shifts in Same-Sex Marriage Attitudes Associated With Declines in Religious Behavior and Affiliation?" *American Politics Research* 51(1): 81–90.

Djupe, Paul A., Jacob R. Neiheisel, and Kimberly H. Conger. 2018. "Are the Politics of the Christian Right Linked to State Rates of the Non-Religious? The Importance of Salient Controversy." *Political Research Quarterly* 71(4): 910–922.

Djupe, Paul A., Jacob R. Neiheisel, and Anand E. Sokhey. 2018. "Reconsidering the Role of Politics in Leaving Religion – The Importance of Affiliation." *American Journal of Political Science* 62 (1): 161–175.

Djupe, Paul A., Anand E. Sokhey, and Christopher P. Gilbert. 2007. "Present but Not Accounted for? Gender Differences in Civic Resource Acquisition." *American Journal of Political Science* 51(4): 906–920.

Edgell, Penny, Joseph Gerteis, and Douglas Hartmann. 2006. "Atheists as 'Other': Moral Boundaries and Cultural Membership in American Society. American Sociological Review 71(2): 211–234.

Edsall, Thomas. 2020. "Trump Is Staking Out His Own Universe of 'Alternative Facts'." *New York Times*. May 13. www.nytimes.com/2020/05/13/opinion/trump-digital-campaign.html. Accessed July 16, 2022.

Edsall, Thomas. 2021. "The Capitol Insurrection Was as Christian Nationalist as It Gets." *New York Times*. January 28. www.nytimes.com/2021/01/28/opinion/christian-nationalists-capitol-attack.html. Accessed July 16, 2022.

Emerson, Michael O. 2022. "What Happens When White Identity Comes before Christian Faith?" *Sojourners*. July. https://sojo.net/magazine/july-2022/what-happens-when-white-identity-comes-christian-faith. Accessed July 18, 2022.

Evans, Geoffrey, and Stephen Whitefield. 1995. "The Politics and Economics of Democratic Commitment: Support for Democracy in Transition Societies." *British Journal of Political Science* 25(4): 485–514.

Fea, John. 2018. *Believe Me*. Grand Rapids, MI: William B. Eerdmans.

Feldman, Max. 2020. "Dirty Tricks: 9 Falsehoods That Could Undermine the 2020 Election." *Brennan Center for Justice*. May 14. www.brennancenter.org/our-work/research-reports/dirty-tricks-9-falsehoods-could-undermine-2020-election. Accessed September 2, 2022.

Feuer, Alan. 2022. "Group Chat Linked to Roger Stone Shows Ties Among Jan. 6 Figures." *New York Times*. May 20. www.nytimes.com/2022/05/20/us/politics/roger-stone-jan-6.html. Accessed August 8, 2022.

Frederiksen, Kristian V. S. 2022. "When Democratic Experience Distorts Democracy: Citizen Reactions to Undemocratic Incumbent Behaviour." *European Journal of Political Research* 61(1): 281–292.

Freedom House. 2021. "NEW REPORT: US Democracy Has Declined Significantly in the Past Decade, Reforms Urgently Needed." March 22. https://freedomhouse.org/article/new-report-us-democracy-has-declined-significantly-past-decade-reforms-urgently-needed. Accessed July 17, 2022.

Frymer, Paul. 1999. *Uneasy Alliances: Race and Party Competition in America*. Princeton, NJ: Princeton University Press.

Friesen, Amanda J., and Paul A. Djupe. 2017. "Conscientious Women under the Stained Glass Ceiling: The Dispositional Conditions of Institutional Treatment on Civic Engagement." *Politics & Gender* 13(1): 57–80.

Gidengill, Elisabeth, Dietlind Stolle, and Olivier Bergeron-Boutin. 2021. "The Partisan Nature of Support for Democratic Backsliding: A comparative Perspective." *European Journal of Political Research* 61(4): 901–929. https://doi.org/10.1111/1475-6765.12502.

Gjelten, Tom. 2021. "A 'Scary' Survey Finding: 4 in 10 Republicans Say Political Violence May Be Necessary." *NPR*. February 11. www.wbur.org/

npr/966498544/a-scary-survey-finding-4-in-10-republicans-say-political-violence-may-be-necessa. Accessed July 17, 2022.

Goldiner, Dave. 2020. "Devilish Comments as Donald Trump Jr. Compares Speaker Pelosi to Satan." *NY Daily News*. February 6. www.nydailynews.com/news/politics/ny-donald-trump-jr-nancy-pelosi-satan-devil-impeachment-20200206-lxcwbzkxjrdf7ncwl4ulwiuruu-story.html. Accessed July 5, 2022.

Goodman, Sara Wallace. 2022. *Citizenship in Hard Times: How Ordinary People Respond to Democratic Threat*. New York: Cambridge University Press.

Goren, Paul, Harald Schoen, Jason Reifler, Thomas Scotto, and William Chittick. 2016. "A Unified Theory of Value-Based Reasoning and US Public Opinion." *Political Behavior* 38(4): 977–997.

Goren, Paul, and Christopher Chapp. 2017. "Moral Power: How Public Opinion on Culture War Issues Shapes Partisan Predispositions and Religious Orientations." *American Political Science Review* 111(1): 110–128.

Gorski, Philip. 2017. *American Covenant: A History of Civil Religion from the Puritans to the Present*. Princeton, NJ: Princeton University Press.

Gorski, Philip S., and Samuel L. Perry. 2022. *The Flag and the Cross: White Christian Nationalism and the Threat to American Democracy*. New York: Oxford University Press.

Graham, Jesse, Jonathan Haidt, and Brian A. Nosek. 2009. "Liberals and Conservatives Rely on Different Sets of Moral Foundations." *Journal of Personality and Social Psychology* 96(5): 1029–1046.

Green Emma. 2015. "How Will the U.S. Supreme Court's Same-Sex Marriage Decision Affect Religious Liberty?" *The Atlantic*. June 26. www.theatlantic.com/politics/archive/2015/06/how-will-the-us-supreme-courts-same-sex-marriage-decision-affect-religious-liberty/396986/. Accessed January 15, 2023

Green, Emma. 2017. "White Evangelicals Believe They Face More Discrimination Than Muslims." *The Atlantic*. March 10. www.theatlantic.com/politics/archive/2017/03/perceptions-discrimination-muslims-christians/519135/. Accessed July 7, 2022.

Green, Emma. 2021. "A Christian Insurrection." *The Atlantic*. January 8. www.theatlantic.com/politics/archive/2021/01/evangelicals-catholics-jericho-march-capitol/617591/.

Green, John C., James L. Guth, Lyman A. Kellstedt, and Corwin E. Smidt. 1994. "Uncivil Challenges: Support for Civil Liberties among Religious Activists." *Journal of Political Science* 22: 25–49.

Griswold, Eliza. 2021. "A Pennsylvania Lawmaker and the Resurgence of Christian Nationalism." www.newyorker.com/news/on-religion/a-pennsylva

nia-lawmaker-and-the-resurgence-of-christian-nationalism. Accessed January 15, 2023.

Grossmann, Matt, and David A. Hopkins. 2016. *Asymmetric Politics: Ideological Republicans and Group Interest Democrats*. New York: Oxford University Press.

Guth, James L., John C. Green, Corwin E. Smidt, Lyman A. Kellstedt, and Margaret Poloma. 1997. *The Bully Pulpit: The Politics of Protestant Clergy*. Lawrence, MA: University of Kansas Press.

Hankins, Barry. 2002. *Uneasy in Babylon: Southern Baptist Conservatives and American Culture*. Tuscaloosa, AL: University of Alabama Press.

Hayes, Danny. 2008. "Does the Messenger Matter? Candidate-Media Agenda Convergence and Its Effects on Voter Issue Salience." *Political Research Quarterly* 61(1): 134–146.

Hibbing, John R., and Elizabeth Theiss-Morse. 2002. *Stealth Democracy*. New York: Cambridge.

Hout, Michael, and Claude S. Fischer. 2002. "Why More Americans Have No Religious Preference: Politics and Generations." *American Sociological Review* 67(2): 165–190.

Hunter, James Davison. 1991. *Culture Wars: The Struggle to Define America*. New York: Basic Books.

Jelen, Ted G., and Clyde Wilcox. 1991. "Religious Dogmatism among White Christians: Causes and Effects." *Review of Religious Research* 33: 32–46.

Jenkins, Jack. 2017. "How Trump's Presidency Reveals the True Nature of Christian Nationalism." *Think Progress*, September 13. https://archive.thinkprogress.org/christian-nationalism-religion-research-b8f9cdc16239/ Accessed April 19, 2023

Jenkins, Jack. 2021. "The Insurrectionists' Senate Floor Prayer Highlights a Curious Trumpian Ecumenism." *Religion News Service*. February 25. https://religionnews.com/2021/02/25/the-insurrectionists-senate-floor-prayer-highlights-a-curious-trumpian-ecumenism/. Accessed July 17, 2022.

Jenkins, Jack. 2022. "How Christian Nationalism Paved the Way for Jan. 6." *Religion News Service*. June 9, 2022: https://religionnews.com/2022/06/09/how-christian-nationalism-paved-the-way-for-january–6/. Accessed January 15, 2023.

Jones, Robert P. 2016. *The End of White Christian America*. New York: Simon & Schuster.

Jones, Robert P. 2019. "The Electoral Time Machine That Could Reelect Trump." *The Atlantic*. June 25. www.theatlantic.com/ideas/archive/2019/06/how-trump-could-win-2020/592354/. Accessed July 5, 2022.

Jones, Robert P. 2021. *White Too Long: The Legacy of White Supremacy in American Christianity*. New York: Simon & Schuster.

Kalmoe, Nathan P., and Lilliana Mason. 2022. *Radical American Partisanship: Mapping Violent Hostility, Its Causes, & What It Means for Democracy*. Chicago: University of Chicago Press.

Kaufmann, Chaim. 2004. "Threat Inflation and the Failure of the Marketplace of Ideas: The Selling of the Iraq War." *International Security* 29(1): 5–48.

Kessler, Glenn. 2020. "The 'Very Fine People' at Charlottesville: Who Were They?" *Washington Post*. May 8. www.washingtonpost.com/politics/2020/05/08/very-fine-people-charlottesville-who-were-they-2/. Accessed July 6, 2022.

Kilgore, ed. 2019. "Christian Right Leaders Suggest Trump Critics are Possessed by Demons." *New York Magazine*. November 26. https://nymag.com/intelligencer/2019/11/christian-right-leaders-trump-critics-possessed-by-demons.html. Accessed Septemeber 2, 2022.

Klar, Samara, and Yanna Krupnikov. 2016. *Independent Politics: How American Disdain for Parties Leads to Political Inaction*. New York: Cambridge.

Kobes du Mez, Kristin. 2020. *Jesus and John Wayne: How White Evangelicals Corrupted a Faith and Fractured a Nation*. New York: Liveright.

Koger, Gregory, Seth Masket, and Hans Noel. 2009. "Partisan Webs: Information Exchange and Party Networks." *British Journal of Political Science* 39(3): 633–653.

Krosnick, Jon A. 1990. "Government Policy and Citizen Passion: A Study of Issue Publics in Contemporary America." *Political Behavior* 12(1): 59–92.

Kruse, Kevin M. 2016. *One Nation Under God: How Corporate America Invented Christian America*. New York: Basic Books.

Lecaque, Thomas. 2022. "The Twisted, Trumpist Religion of Jan. 6th. *The Bulwark*. January 6. www.thebulwark.com/the-twisted-trumpist-religion-of-jan-6th/. Accessed January 15, 2023.

Layman, Geoffrey. 2001. *The Great Divide: Religious and Cultural Conflict in American Party Politics*. New York: Columbia University Press.

Layman, Geoffrey, and Mark Brockway. 2018. "Evangelical Activists in the GOP: Still the Life of the Party? In *The Evangelical Crackup? The Future of the Evangelical-Republican Coalition*. Paul A. Djupe and Ryan L. Claassen, eds., 32–48. Philadelphia, PA: Temple University Press.

Layman, Geoffrey, and Thomas M. Carsey. 2002. "Party Polarization and 'Conflict Extension' in the American Electorate." *American Journal of Political Science* 46(4): 786–802.

Leege, David C., Kenneth D. Wald, and Brian S. Krueger. 2002. *The Politics of Cultural Differences: Social Change and Voter Mobilization Strategies in the Post-New Deal Period*. Princeton, NJ: Princeton University Press.

Levitsky, Steven, and Daniel Ziblatt. 2018. *How Democracies Die*. New York: Crown.

Lewis, Andrew R. 2014. "Abortion Politics and the Decline of the Separation of Church and State: The Southern Baptist Case." *Politics and Religion* 7(3): 521–549.

Lewis, Andrew R. 2017. *The Rights Turn in Conservative Christian Politics: How Abortion Transformed the Culture Wars*. New York: Cambridge University Press.

Lewis, Andrew R. 2019. "The Inclusion-Moderation Thesis: The US Republican Party and the Christian Right," In *Oxford Research Encyclopedia of Politics*. Djupe, Paul A., Mark J. Rozell, and Ted G. Jelen, eds., 635–650. New York: Oxford University Press.

Lewis, Andrew R. 2021. "Christian Nationalism and the Remaking of Religion and Politics." *Sociology of Religion* 82(1): 111–115.

Lewis, Andrew R. 2022. "The New Supreme Court Doctrine against Religious Discrimination." *The Washington Post*. July 7. www.washingtonpost.com/politics/2022/07/07/scotus-carson-makin-maine-schools-bremerton-football-coach/. Accessed January 15, 2023.

Lewis, Andrew R., and Daniel Bennett. 2023. "Precedent, Performance, and Polarization: The Christian Legal Movement and Religious Freedom Politics during the Coronavirus Pandemic." In *'An Epidemic among My People': Religion in the Age of COVID-19*. Paul A. Djupe and Amanda J. Friesen, eds., 99–110. Philadelphia, PA: Temple University Press.

Lewis, Andrew R., and Eric L. McDaniel. Forthcoming. "Religious Freedom Backlash: Evidence from Public Opinion Experiments about Free Expression." *PS: Political Science & Politics* 56(2): 227–233. https://doi.org/10.1017/S1049096522001251.

Lundberg, Matthew D. 2021. *Christian Martyrdom and Christian Violence: On Suffering and Wielding the Sword*. New York: Oxford University Press.

Lupia, Arthur, and Matthew D. McCubbins. 1998. *The Democratic Dilemma: Can Citizens Learn What They Need to Know*. New York: Cambridge University Press.

Mantyla, Kyle. 2019a. "'Satan Hates This Man': Perry Stone Says Trump's Critics 'Have Demons in Them'." *Right Wing Watch*. October 28. www.rightwingwatch.org/post/satan-hates-this-man-perry-stone-says-trumps-critics-have-demons-in-them/. Accessed July 5, 2022.

Mantyla, Kyle. 2019b. "Ralph Reed: Christians Deserve Persecution if They Fail to Reelect Trump in 2020." *Right Wing Watch.* November 5. https://www.rightwingwatch.org/post/ralph-reed-christians-deserve-persecution-if-they-fail-to-reelect-trump-in-2020/ Accessed May 28, 2021.

Margolis, Michele F. 2018. *From Politics to the Pews: How Partisanship and the Political Environment Shape Religious Identity.* Chicago, IL: University of Chicago Press.

Martínez, Jessica, and Gregory A. Smith. 2016. "How the Faithful Voted: A Preliminary 2016 Analysis." *Pew Research Center.* November 9. www.pewresearch.org/fact-tank/2016/11/09/how-the-faithful-voted-a-preliminary-2016-analysis/. Accessed January 15, 2023.

Mason, Lilliana H. 2018. *Uncivil Agreement: How Politics Became Our Identity.* Chicago, IL: University of Chicago Press.

Mason, Lilliana H., and Julie Wronski. 2018. "One Tribe to Bind Them All: How Our Social Group Attachments Strengthen Partisanship." *Political Psychology* 39(S1): 257–277.

Maxwell, Angie, and Todd Shields. 2019. *The Long Southern Strategy: How Chasing White Voters in the South Changed American Politics.* New York: Oxford University Press.

McAfee, Tierney. 2018. "Evangelical Leader Says Trump Gets 'a Mulligan' on Alleged Affair with Porn Star." *Yahoo.* January 24. www.yahoo.com/entertainment/evangelical-leader-says-trump-gets-172953748.html. Accessed July 16, 2022.

McCarty, Nolan. 2019. *Polarization: What Everyone Needs to Know.* New York: Oxford University Press.

McDaniel, Eric L., Irfan Nooruddin, and Allyson Faith Shortle. 2011. "Divine Boundaries: How Religion Shapes Citizens' Attitudes Toward Immigrants." *American Politics Research* 39(1): 205–233.

McDaniel, Eric L., Irfan Nooruddin, and Allyson Faith Shortle. 2022: *The Everyday Crusade: Christian Nationalism in American Politics.* New York: Cambridge University Press.

Miller, Joanne M., and Jon A. Krosnick. 2004. "Threat as a Motivator of Political Activism: A Field Experiment." *Political Psychology* 25(4): 507–523.

Moskalenko, Sophia, and Clark McCauley. 2009. "Measuring Political Mobilization: The Distinction between Activism and Radicalism." *Terrorism and Political Violence* 21: 239–260.

Moss, Candida. 2013. *The Myth of Persecution: How Early Christians Invented a Story of Martyrdom.* New York: HarperCollins.

Navarre, Brianna. 2021. "U.S. Democracy Is 'Backsliding,' For First Time, Study Says." *US New and World Report. November* 24. www.usnews.com/

news/best-countries/articles/2021-11-24/study-classifies-u-s-democracy-as-backsliding-for-the-first-time. Accessed July 17, 2022.

Noble, Alan. 2014. "The Evangelical Persecution Complex." *The Atlantic*. August 4. www.theatlantic.com/national/archive/2014/08/the-evangelical-persecution-complex/375506/. Accessed July 5, 2022.

Norris, Pippa. 2011. "Does Democratic Satisfaction Reflect Regime Performance?" *How Democracy Works: Political Representation and Policy Congruence in Modern Societies*. Martin Rosema, Bas Denters, and Kees Arts. ed., 115–136. Amsterdam: Amsterdam University Press,.

Nunn, Clyde Z., Harry J. Crocket, Jr., and J. Allen Williams, Jr. 1978. *Tolerance for Non-Conformists*. San Francisco, CA: Jossey-Bass.

O'Harrow, Robert, Andrew Ba Tran, and Derek Hawkins 2021. "The Rise of Domestic Extremism in America." *Washington Post*. April 12. www .washingtonpost.com/investigations/interactive/2021/domestic-terrorism-data/. Accessed July 27, 2022.

Onishi, Bradley. 2023. *Preparing for War: The Extremist History of White Christian Nationalism –and What Comes Next*. Minneapolis, MN: Broadleaf Books.

Owen, Dennis E., Kenneth D. Wald, and Samuel S. Hill. 1991. "Authoritarian or Authority-Minded? The Cognitive Commitments of Fundamentalists and the Christian Right." *Religion and American Culture: A Journal of Interpretation* 1(1): 73–100.

Pape, Robert A. 2021. "Understanding the American Insurrectionist Movement: A Nationally Representative Survey." *Chicago Project on Security and Threats*.https://d3qi0qp55mx5f5.cloudfront.net/cpost/i/docs/ CPOST-NORC_UnderstandingInsurrectionSurvey_JUN2021_Topline.pdf.

Patrikios, Stratos. 2013. "Self-Stereotyping as 'Evangelical Republican': An Empirical Test." *Politics & Religion* 6(4): 800–822.

Perry, Samuel L., and Andrew L. Whitehead. 2022. "January 6th May Have Been Only the First Wave of Christian Nationalist Violence." *Time Magazine*. January 4. https://time.com/6132591/january-6th-christian-nationalism/. Accessed July 17, 2022.

Perry, Samuel L., and Andrew L. Whitehead. 2021. "Racialized Religion and Judicial Injustice: How Whiteness and Biblicist Christianity Intersect to Promote a Preference for (Unjust) Punishment." *Journal for the Scientific Study of Religion* 60(1): 46–63.

Perry, Samuel L., Andrew L. Whitehead, and Joshua T. Davis. 2019. "God's Country in Black and Blue: How Christian Nationalism Shapes Americans' Views about Police (Mis)treatment of Blacks." *Sociology of Race and Ethnicity* 5(1):130–146.

Perry, Samuel L., and Andrew L. Whitehead. 2015. "Christian Nationalism, Racial Separatism, and Family Formation: Attitudes toward Transracial Adoption as a Test Case. " *Race and Social Problems* 7(2):123–134.

Perry, Samuel L., Joseph Baker, and Joshua Grubbs. 2021. "Ignorance or Culture War? Christian Nationalism and Scientific Illiteracy." *Public Understanding of Science* 30(8): 930–946. https://doi.org/10.1177/09636625211006271.

Petersen, Michael B., Rune Slothuus, Rune Stubager, and Lise Togeby. 2011. "Freedom for All? The Strength and Limits of Political Tolerance." *British Journal of Political Science* 41(3): 581–597.

Petrocik, John R., William L. Benoit, and Glenn J. Hansen. 2003. "Issue Ownership and Presidential Campaigning, 1952–2000." *Political Science Quarterly* 118(4): 599–626.

Pietryka, Matthew T., and Randall C. MacIntosh. 2022. "ANES Scales Often Do Not Measure What You Think They Measure." *Journal of Politics* 84(2): 1074–1090.

Pratto, Felicia, James Sidanius, Lisa M. Stallworth, and Bertram F. Malle. 1994. "Social Dominance Orientation: A Personality Variable Predicting Social and Political Attitudes." *Journal of Personality and Social Psychology* 67(4): 741–763.

Primoratz, Igor. 2020. "Patriotism." *The Stanford Encyclopedia of Philosophy* (Winter 2020 Edition). Edward N. Zalta, ed. https://plato.stanford.edu/archives/win2020/entries/patriotism/.

Reimer, Sam, and Jerry Z. Park. 2001. "Tolerant Incivility: A Longitudinal Analysis of White Conservative Protestants' Willingness to Grant Civil Liberties." *Journal for the Scientific Study of Religion* 40(4): 735–745.

Reny, Tyler, Bryan Wilcox-Alchuleta, and Vanessa Cruz Nichols. 2019. "Threat, Mobilization, and Latino Voting in the 2018 Election." *The Forum* 16(4): 631–657.

Rizzo, Salvador. 2019. "President Trump's Shifting Claim That 'We Got Rid' of the Johnson Amendment." *Washington Post*. May 9. www.washingtonpost.com/politics/2019/05/09/president-trumps-shifting-claim-that-we-got-rid-johnson-amendment/. Accessed July 15, 2022.

Rorty, Richard. 1994. "Religion as Conversation-stopper." *Common Knowledge* 3 (1): 1–6.

Rose, Richard, and William Mishler. 1996. "Testing the Churchill Hypothesis: Popular Support for Democracy and Its Alternatives." *Journal of Public Policy* 16(1): 29–58.

Rosenstone, Steven J., and John Mark Hansen. 1993. *Mobilization, Participation, and Democracy in America*. New York: Macmillan.

Rosin, Hanna. 1999. "Columbine Miracle: A Matter of Belief." *Washington Post*. October 14. www.washingtonpost.com/wp-srv/WPcap/1999-10/14/026r-101499-idx.html. Accessed July 5, 2022.

Rozell, Mark J., and Clyde Wilcox, eds. 1995. *God at the Grassroots: The Christian Right in the 1994 Elections*. Lanham, MD: Rowman and Littlefield.

Schwadel, Philip, and Christopher R. H. Garneau. 2019. "Sectarian Religion and Political Tolerance in the United States." *Sociology of Religion* 80(2): 168–193.

Schwartz, Shalom H. 2007. "Cultural and Individual Value Correlates of Capitalism: A Comparative Analysis." *Psychological Inquiry* 18(1): 52–57.

Scott, Eugene. 2017. "Trump Says He's Fulfilled His Promises to Christians, but He Really Means White Evangelicals." *Washington Post*. October 14. www.washingtonpost.com/news/the-fix/wp/2017/10/15/trump-says-hes-fulfilled-his-promises-to-christians-but-he-really-means-white-evangelicals/. Accessed July 5, 2022.

Shaffner, Brian F. 2022. "The Heightened Importance of Racism and Sexism in the 2018 US Midterm Elections." *British Journal of Political Science* 52: 492–500.

Sherkat, Darren E., and Derek Lehman. 2018. "Bad Samaritans: Religion and Anti-Immigrant and Anti-Muslim Sentiment in the United States" *Social Science Quarterly* 99: 1791–1804.

Shortle, Allyson F., and Ronald Keith Gaddie. 2015. "Religious Nationalism and Perceptions of Muslims and Islam." *Politics and Religion* 8(3): 435–457.

Sides, John, Michael Tesler, and Lynn Vavreck. 2019. *Identity Crisis*. Princeton, NJ: Princeton University Press.

Smietana, Bob. 2021. "Jericho March Returns to DC to Pray for a Trump Miracle." *Christianity Today*. January 5. www.christianitytoday.com/news/2021/january/jericho-march-dc-election-overturn-trump-biden-congress.html. Accessed January 15, 2023.

Smidt, Corwin, and James M. Penning. 1982. "Religious Commitment, Political Conservatism, and Political and Social Tolerance in the United States: A Longitudinal Analysis." *Sociological Analysis* 43: 231–246.

Smidt, Corwin E. 2016. *Pastors and Public Life: The Changing Face of American Protestant Clergy*. New York: Oxford University Press.

Smith, Christian. 1998. *American Evangelicalism: Embattled and Thriving*. Chicago, IL: University of Chicago Press.

Smith, Steven B. 2021. *Reclaiming Patriotism in an Age of Extremes*. New Haven, CT: Yale University Press.

Soper, J. Christopher, and Joel S. Fetzer. 2018. *Religion and Nationalism in Global Perspective*. New York: Cambridge University Press.

SPLC. 2019. "Hate Groups Reach Record High." *Southern Poverty Law Center*. February 19. www.splcenter.org/news/2019/02/19/hate-groups-reach-record-high. Accessed July 27, 2022.

Sprunt, Barbara. 2022. "Jan. 6 Panel Show Evidence of Coordination between Far-Right Groups and Trump Allies." *NPR*. July 12. www.npr.org/2022/07/12/1111132464/jan-6-hearing-recap-oath-keepers-proud-boys. Accessed January 15, 2023.

Stewart, Katherine. 2020. *The Power Worshippers: Inside the Dangerous Rise of Religious Nationalism*. London: Bloomsbury.

Stewart, Katherine. 2022. "Christian Nationalists are Excited about What Comes Next." *New York Times*. July 5. www.nytimes.com/2022/07/05/opinion/dobbs-christian-nationalism.html. Accessed July 5, 2022.

Sullivan, John L., James Piereson, and George E. Marcus. 1982. *Political Tolerance and American Democracy*. Chicago, IL: University of Chicago Press.

Taylor, Charles. 2002. "Democracy, Inclusive and Exclusive." In *Meaning and Modernity: Religion, Polity and the Self*, R. Madsen, W. Sullivan, A. Swidler, and S. Tipton, eds. 181–194. Berkeley, CA: University of California Press.

Thrall, A. Trevor. 2007. "A Bear in the Woods? Threat Framing and the Marketplace of Values." *Security Studies* 16(3): 452–488.

Vegter, Abigail, Andrew R. Lewis, and Cammie Jo Bolin. 2023. "Which Civil Religion? Partisanship, Christian Nationalism, and the Dimensions of Civil Religion in the United States." *Politics and Religion* 16(2).

Verba, Sidney, Kay Lehman Schlozman, and Henry E. Brady. 1995. *Voice and Equality: Civic Voluntarism in American Politics*. Cambridge, MA: Harvard University Press.

Victory Channel. No date. "Atlanta Declaration." https://flashpoint.govictory.com/atlanta-declaration/. Accessed July 5, 2022.

Washington Post. 2020. "Exit Poll Results and Analysis for the 2020 Presidential Election." December 14, 2020: www.washingtonpost.com/elections/interactive/2020/exit-polls/presidential-election-exit-polls/. January 15, 2023.

Wehner, Peter. 2019. "Are Trump's Critics Demonically Possessed?" *The Atlantic*. November 5. www.theatlantic.com/ideas/archive/2019/11/to-trumps-evangelicals-everyone-else-is-a-sinner/602569/. Accessed July 5, 2022.

Weisman, Jonathan, and Reid J. Epstein. 2022. "G.O.P. Declares Jan. 6 Attack 'Legitimate Political Discourse'." *The New York Times*. February 4, 2022. www.nytimes.com/2022/02/04/us/politics/republicans-jan-6-cheney-censure.html. Accessed July 16, 2022.

Westwood, Sean .J., Justin Grimmer, Matthew Tyler, and Clayton Nall. 2022. "Current Research Overstates American Support for Political Violence." *Proceedings of the National Academy of Sciences*, *119*(12), e2116870119.

Whitehead, Andrew L., and Samuel L. Perry. 2015. "A More Perfect Union? Christian Nationalism and Support for Same-sex Unions." *Sociological Perspectives* 58(3): 422–440.

Whitehead, Andrew L., and Samuel L. Perry. 2020a. *Taking America Back for God: Christian Nationalism in the United States*. New York: Oxford University Press.

Whitehead, Andrew L., and Samuel L. Perry. 2020b. "How Culture Wars Delay Herd Immunity: Christian Nationalism and Anti-vaccine Attitudes." *Socius: Sociological Research for a Dynamic World* 6: 1–12.

Whitehead, Andrew L., Samuel L. Perry, and Joshua B. Grubbs. 2023. "Christian Nationalism and the COVID-19 Pandemic." In *"An Epidemic Among My People": Religion in the Age of COVID-19*. Paul A. Djupe and Amanda J. Friesen, eds. Philadelphia, PA: Temple University Press.

Whitehead, Andrew L., Landon Schnabel, and Samuel L. Perry. 2018. "Gun Control in the Crosshairs: Christian Nationalism and Opposition to Stricter Gun Laws." *Socius* 4: 1–13.

Wilkinson, Alissa. 2019. "After Columbine, Martyrdom became a Powerful Fantasy for ChristianTeenagers." *Vox*. April 20. www.vox.com/culture/2017/4/20/15369442/columbine-anniversary-cassie-bernall-rachel-scott-martyrdom. Accessed July 5, 2022.

Wilson, Angelia R., and Paul A. Djupe. 2020. "Communicating in Good Faith? Dynamics of the Christian Right Agenda." *Politics & Religion* 13(2): 385–414.

Wingfield, Mark. 2021. "Pastors Respond to Unbelievable Events at Capitol on Epiphany 2021." *Baptist News*. January 7. https://baptistnews.com/article/pastors-respond-to-unbelievable-events-at-capitol-on-epiphany-2021/. Accessed July 16, 2022.

Winston, Kimberly. 2021. "The History behind the Christian Flags Spotted at the Pro-Trump U.S. Capitol 'Coup.'" *Religion Unplugged*. January 6. https://religionunplugged.com/news/2021/1/6/some-history-behind-the-christian-flags-at-the-pro-trump-capitol-coup.

Zaller, John R. 1992. *The Nature and Origins of Mass Opinion*. New York: Cambridge University Press.

# Acknowledgments

This Element was only possible because of the sustained efforts of a group of scholars who worked together, shook their couch cushions, and cobbled together survey after survey for a number of years. We live in a golden age of public opinion research, with access never easier, but it is still a barrier that most individual academics have trouble hurdling. We are grateful to have extensive coauthor and colleague networks with modest collective action dispositions to make this work, including Jason Adkins, Ryan Burge, Ryan Claassen, Amanda Friesen, Jake Neiheisel, and John Ryan. Most of the sources of those funds were (small) individual research accounts, but some institutions deserve mention, including the Louisville Institute and the Institute for Humane Studies, which provided grants to collect survey data. We also benefited from conversations with Nick Davis, Sam Perry, Andrew Whitehead, Eric McDaniel, the American Politics Research Lab at CU, and participants of panels at APSA, MPSA, and FRAPSA. We are also grateful to Cambridge University Press, and especially the Elements in American Politics series editor, Frances Lee, for believing in this project.

# Cambridge Elements ≡

## American Politics

### Elements in the Series

*Red, Green, and Blue: The Partisan Divide on Environmental Issues*
David Karol

*Contemporary US Populism in Comparative Perspective*
Kirk Hawkins and Levente Littvay

*False Alarm: The Truth about Political Mistruths in the Trump Era*
Ethan Porter and Thomas J. Wood

*Converging on Truth: A Dynamic Perspective on Factual Debates in American Public Opinion*
James A. Stimson and Emily Wager

*The Acceptance and Expression of Prejudice During the Trump Era*
Brian F. Schaffner

*American Affective Polarization in Comparative Perspective*
Noam Gidron, James Adams and Will Horne

*The Study of US State Policy Diffusion: What Hath Walker Wrought?*
Christopher Z. Mooney

*Why Bad Policies Spread (and Good Ones Don't)*
Charles R. Shipan and Craig Volden

*The Partisan Next Door: Stereotypes of Party Supporters and Consequences for Polarization in America*
Ethan C. Busby, Adam J. Howat, Jacob E. Rothschild and Richard M. Shafranek

*The Dynamics of Public Opinion*
Mary Layton Atkinson, K. Elizabeth Coggins, James A. Stimson and Frank R. Baumgartner

*The Origins and Consequences of Congressional Party Election Agendas*
Scott R. Meinke

*The Full Armor of God: The Mobilization of Christian Nationalism in American Politics*
Paul A. Djupe, Andrew R. Lewis and Anand E. Sokhey

A full series listing is available at: www.cambridge.org/core/series/elements-in-american-politics

Printed in the United States
by Baker & Taylor Publisher Services